Eugene O'Neill

EUGENE O'NEILL

by Olivia Coolidge

CHARLES SCRIBNER'S SONS   NEW YORK

Photograph for jacket and frontispiece courtesy Culver Pictures, Inc.

CONTENTS

INTRODUCTION

EUGENE O'NEILL is as American as he is Irish. He represents to us not the old traditions of North or South, nor yet the pioneer West. His America is even bigger than these. It is the country of the immigrant, of the man who has lost his background and must fight to win a home in an unfamiliar world. Typically, O'Neill is both resentful and avid. He wants success in the American struggle, even while denouncing its soulless materialism. Casting aside his traditional beliefs, he fumbles for new ones. Sympathy for others in the same predicament he certainly feels, yet his war with society is always a personal effort. Politics, sociology, philanthropy he leaves to others. O'Neill has something to say because his life represents, even exaggerates the sufferings of that tremendous human flood which spilled out of Europe into the land of opportunity.

O'Neill is a man who has lost his rudder. His works are on a great scale, as is fitting considering the greatness of our country, the size of its migrations, and the life-and-death struggle which engulfed so many. Yet both as a man and a writer, he was not consistently above life-size. It is hard to understand how a man so capable of sympathy could be so remote, how a writer of such emotional power can be so lacking in basic eloquence, how a genius could lower himself to become a down-and-out and helpless drunkard. Yet in the world which he represents, great faults are the complement of great achievements. Progress is not smooth. Reactions are exaggerated, first in one direction, then in another. It is the turmoil of a whole generation that we behold in O'Neill.

All his major characters are creatures of passion, unable to dominate forces which they do not understand. They are lost in a world which is too big for them. It matters little that their struggle is not with an everyday world but an inner one. The genius of O'Neill has lifted their conflict onto an emotional plane, but their defeat represents that of many thousands, of millions perhaps who came over from the old country, only to discover that they were not strong enough to control their destiny.

Typical he may be, but at the same time O'Neill is

intensely individual. One could hardly imagine a life and background more unlike that of the common herd. The family history of the O'Neills is a lurid melodrama which seems at first sight too improbable to carry conviction. Nor does O'Neill's personality fit into any of the categories we may have waiting for him. The same thing is true of his writings. They have been liked and disliked, admired, despised, and all with reason. But however they are regarded, they must be reckoned with. They can never be ignored. Here again O'Neill is like his age. It had vitality, and so does he.

Without a knowledge of O'Neill's world, of his inheritance, and of his life, it would be impossible to understand his dramas to the full. We need to know what forces drove him, all the more so because he is not always himself completely certain what they are or where he is going. Besides, his history concerns us directly. His generation was only yesterday's. It has shaped today and will influence tomorrow. His dramas reflect both how he lived and what he saw. Through them we see O'Neill, and through O'Neill America.

1   A MOMENT OF BIRTH

PROVINCETOWN, MASSACHUSETTS, lies on the tip of Cape
Cod, nestling inside the crooked finger of land which
curves into the Atlantic. It mainly consists of two parallel
streets, each three miles long and gently twisting to fit
the shape of the great bay. In fact, all Provincetown looks
out across its magnificent harbor, large enough to shelter a
vast fleet. There is no other way for the town to turn.
Behind lie the dunes where life and death meet in perpetual struggle in the shape of coarse beach grass and

shifting sand. On these in winter storms the fierce Atlantic has cast up many a corpse, for the coast is dangerous. Even in summer the dunes are lonely places. Not so Provincetown. Today, a new speed highway has opened up Cape Cod. Beach cottages and motels have massed themselves nowhere more thickly than in the approaches to Provincetown. On Commerce Street, every shop sells curios, every dwelling is hotel, boardinghouse, or outright residence for summer visitors. Natives there are, both Yankee and Portuguese, burned brown by sun and wind. But these stand out more clearly than their dwellings, which do not push aside the tourist clutter until the season is gone and half of Provincetown is frankly boarded up. Then it may be seen that the sometimes dingy oases of life in the town have character. It has been greatly eroded by the flood of tourism, but it may still remind us that the past of Provincetown is not inglorious. Around 1900 the little town manned a sailing fleet of over two hundred and fifty, which included whalers, schooners fishing the Grand Banks for cod, and coasting vessels.

Times change fast, not always for the better. Refrigeration and steam ruined Provincetown as a fishing center. Traffic in fresh fish passed to Boston, where transport facilities were greater. Steam trawlers with new techniques superseded the dories and fishing schooners of Provincetown captains. By 1916, the heyday of Provincetown was over. To be sure, whale vertebrae and curious shells still adorned the native gardens. Flowers were planted in old dories. Perhaps thirty of the town's wharves were still standing, not all in active use. But the summer folk were here as well. The arrival of the season's first excursion boat was saluted by every siren and foghorn in the harbor. Barkers were standing outside restaurants; advertising banners hung across the sandy, unpaved street.

For the summer folk, this was Provincetown's most attractive period. It had still the simplicity of a fisherman's town. They themselves were few in number and intimate with one another. Rents were cheap, houses going for a song. George Cram Cook and his wife, Susan Glaspell, who were certainly far from well-to-do, had bought themselves one. It was a low, narrow house standing sideways to Commercial Street and typical of Provincetown in that it was not built for a view. Everybody saw all of the sea he desired in daily life. On the seaward side of Commerce Street were the wharves, the yards, the smell of fish and tar, the smithying, the coopering—all the noises of the trades that service ships. The Cook house looked at its own yard, save through the parlor windows, where one might peer past an old ship chandler's and wharf behind it, then owned by Mary Heaton Vorse O'Brien, through whom the Cooks had come to Provincetown.

In the summer of 1916, in that front parlor of the Cooks, a group of close friends were gathered to listen while one of their number read aloud a one-act play. It was called *Bound East for Cardiff*; and the author was a young Mr. O'Neill of Irish extraction and evidently in his middle twenties. He was tallish, lean, extremely dark, wore a somber expression and a little black mustache. Painfully nervous and shy, he had refused to be present while they read his work. He had retired to the dining room next door, no doubt assuming the sulky air with which he habitually concealed his sensitiveness to criticism.

The occasion was recognized afterwards, if not at the time, as being momentous in the literal sense in which a battle is momentous. It altered history. It is easy to point out that if a flood is damned up in one place, it will escape in another. If American drama had not been born in Provincetown in 1916, it would have been born somewhere, some time, and soon. One might as well say that if Napoleon had won at Waterloo, he would have been defeated somewhere, sometime, and soon. France had not the resources to carry on the struggle very much longer. Yet no one suggests that Waterloo was not crucial. The fact is that the importance of an incident is not diminished merely because it was bound to happen. What concerns the historian is not how it might have occurred, but how it did.

George Cook, or Jig to his friends, had got a group together to present a few one-act plays they had written themselves. No one of them was in a professional sense a dramatist. Wilbur Daniel Steele and Susan Glaspell were novelists and magazine writers. Hutchins Hapgood, Max Eastman, Jack Reed, and others were newspaper men. The Zorachs and Charles Demuth were artists. Jig Cook himself was an artistic Jack-of-all-trades, and decidedly master of none.

Nearest to professional were the actors Ed and Stella Ballantine and Ida Rauh, Max Eastman's wife, who, though she had trained as a lawyer, had helped to found a little theater in New York in order to present better plays than were to be seen on Broadway. Ida Rauh had acted with the Washington Square Players for part of a season when her career was cut short by an unfortunate incident. She was cast in the leading role in a small satirical drama by Lawrence Langner, one of the moving spirits and financial backers of the scheme. A bridegroom had died on his wedding day, and the bride's family were trying to get her married to the corpse. The scene opened with the dead man stretched on a couch covered up by a sheet, while Ida as the bride posed weeping beside him. Unluckily, the corpse sat up to rearrange his covers, not realizing that the curtain had just risen. The audience naturally roared with laughter. Ida called for the curtain to be run down; and then she refused to appear on the stage. The whole effect, she said, was ruined. The audience would laugh whenever it saw her. After a long and heated altercation, she was persuaded that the show must go on. By now the delay had made the audience restive, and the play was not a success. Langner did not forgive her. She parted from the Washington Square Players and, among the amateurs in Provincetown, ranked as an actress.

Though the group was amateur, however, it was not an ordinary one. All its members were artists of some sort, and nearly all were writers. They were people who were accustomed to believe that their thoughts mattered. The last dozen years had been times of ferment in America. New notions of social reform had been long one of the exports to America from Europe. Only recently, however, had these foreign ideas attracted the interest of people brought up in traditional American families. To the intellectuals of 1916, new thoughts on the condition of the poor, the emancipation of women, socialism, religion, and marriage had become the fashion. As is sometimes the case when ideas are plentiful, optimism was in the air. It looked easy to sweep cobwebs away and make a fresh start. Even the terrible conflict of World War I taking place in Europe was only beginning to impress the American mind. War seemed contrary to reason, typical of old Europe, and without message for a generation which was pressing forward to bring in a new age.

George Cook and his friends had met in Greenwich Village in New York. The district was taking its place as the chief center of new ideas in American life. The Provincetown summer visitors were not, in other words, followers of fashion. They were among its creators and exercised an influence on public opinion out of all proportion to their individual abilities. Anything they did as a group was invested with importance. When they turned their attention to drama, they might not all do so at first out of any sense of mission; and yet they expected to make some stir. Nor would it have surprised them if one or two of their number had turned out to have talent of a dramatic kind. It was more astonishing, perhaps, to recognize this in young Mr. O'Neill with his trunk full of unsuccessful plays. Yet Greenwich Village had many brilliant people who turned up from unexpected places. Why should not one appear in Provincetown?

For all these reasons, the Provincetown group hailed O'Neill with enthusiasm. Undoubtedly some felt no more than passing pleasure. Others, if Susan Glaspell is to be believed, saw further. "Then we knew," she wrote long after, "what we were for." Her memories may have been distorted by what followed. It seems more likely, however, that she was right. Jig Cook, her husband, knew a good deal about drama. He recognized the chance fate was offering him.

The vision of George Cram Cook may be less important than the genius of O'Neill, but it had its influence on the revolution which took place in American drama. Both men were born of their times and were thinking in what were then modern terms. Each needed the other. Without the Provincetown Players, it is hard to be certain that much would have been heard of O'Neill. He might so easily have drunk himself to death in black despair. Without O'Neill, we may be positive that nothing would have come of the Provincetown Players. George Cram Cook would have been just another failure, lamented only by a few of his intimate friends, who thought that he was bigger and better than his powers of artistic expression. As it is, he made for himself a niche in history. Biographers of O'Neill must mention his name. In the evolution of American drama, he has his modest place. His achievement looks greater now than that of friends whose little novels were published at the time and well reviewed.

2   THE MAKING OF EUGENE O'NEILL

THE SILENT, gloomy young man who wrote *Bound East for Cardiff* was the product of an upbringing which was strangely distorted. His parents, children of Irish immigrants, had soared far above the ugly beginnings which the first generation had made in city slums. Prosperous, even to some extent cultured, they had retained their ancient faith and simple values. Their mutual devotion was unquestioned. Their family feelings were profound. Yet in this promising soil there lurked strange seeds. Eugene

O'Neill's dramas are intensely personal. They chronicle a wild attempt to escape from a background which literally haunts him. But though he turns away, he also turns back, probing and analyzing as though the scars of suffering could in this way be erased. In fact, he wrote of his family all his life.

It is easy to pile up instances to prove that knowledge of O'Neill's family is fundamental to the understanding of all his plays. He gave, for instance, the names and to some extent the relationships of his parents to a Negro boy and a white girl in *All God's Chillun Got Wings*. He allowed himself in *Ah, Wilderness!* a gentle smile for the kind of youth he might have had. The Miller family, as unlike his own as it could be, lived in the O'Neills' New London house complete to a detail. As he grew older, he turned back even more firmly into the past, portraying his family more for the purpose of laying old ghosts than with the intention of bringing out deep tragic meaning. *A Long Day's Journey Into Night* is a piece of autobiography more revealing than many a man's reminiscences not cast in fictional form. A companion to this play, *A Moon for the Misbegotten*, gives a picture of his brother Jamie. For the last years of his life he was working on a great series about the migration of a family from Ireland to America. In short, the major preoccupation of his life for his last ten years was the unhappiness which his family had passed on to him and which he in turn handed down to his children.

James O'Neill, who had been brought to this country in 1856 at nine years old, was the son of poor Irish immigrants who settled in Cincinnati. His father soon gave up the struggle in the new country. He had a vision, he said, calling him back to Ireland to die. He left behind him a widow and six children to look after themselves.

Some grim years followed. Two older boys drifted away from home, leaving James at ten or eleven the man of the family. He got work in a machinist's shop twelve hours a day. His mother went out as a cleaning woman. His elder sister took in sewing. Such jobs were precarious and underpaid. Hunger must have been familiar enough, while the dread of starvation was ever-present in times when no public assistance lightened the lot of the unemployed poor. James never forgot those days, though he made little of them when romancing about his past. They did not lend themselves to colorful pictures.

Luckily for him, his sister made a good match. Her husband gave James a chance to get more education and put by a little money. By 1867, at twenty-one years old, he was looking about him for an opportunity. His savings had been almost used up by unsuccessful ventures, but he was already known as a genial soul in the local saloons, or poor man's clubs, of Cincinnati. Like other lads his age, he loved the theater, but without any thought of an acting career. However, as he was playing billiards one day and waiting for the theater to open, the manager of the stage extras came in, looking for help. His people had gone on strike, and the young man got a chance to walk on-stage. The play being acted was *Colleen Bawn*, an Irish comedy which exactly suited James. The magic of the stage excited him. His appearance, which was striking, pleased the manager. James stayed on for twenty-five cents a night and was

soon promoted to general utility man. From this he graduated to speaking parts and began to move up in the
world. He joined traveling companies, learned his trade the
hard way, and attracted the attention of established actors.

James O'Neill had enthusiasm and was willing to
work. Nature had given him black curls, splendid dark
eyes, classical features, fine white teeth, a good carriage. He
was also endowed with a great organlike voice and a rich
brogue. He took immense trouble with these, learning
painstakingly to control the first and eliminate the second.
He read Shakespeare and the literature of the theater. He
studied fencing, indispensable in romantic roles. Soon he
was taking leading roles in minor companies. Eventually he
rose to play Othello and Iago on alternate nights with
Edwin Booth. At thirty he made his debut in a good stock
company in New York. He did not please the critics yet,
but the public enjoyed him. He was still rising and meant
to reach the top. It was at this point that he married
Ellen Quinlan.

She was eleven years younger than he, also the daugh-
ter of Irish immigrants. But whereas James's early life had
been hard, Ella's was easy. Her father, who had settled in
Cleveland, prospered in various enterprises, particularly
through a liquor store and some real-estate investments.
Ella was given every advantage. As she showed musical
talent, her father had her well taught and bought a piano.
At fifteen, he sent her to St. Mary's Convent at Notre
Dame, Indiana. Few colleges admitted women as yet, but
St. Mary's offered a good education compared to that of
most girls' schools. In particular, its music department was
excellent. Mother Elizabeth, who ran it, had been edu-

cated in Europe and was more than qualified to judge
Ella's talent, which she thought was considerable. The girl
herself was well-behaved; and the nuns found no special
fault with her, save that, like most adolescents, she was
emotional. In fact, she felt she had a sort of vision, a call
to be a nun. Mother Elizabeth demurred. Why did not
Ella wait for a couple of years after leaving school and
think things over? Her foresight was justified. Before two
years were up, Ella was married.

She had already met James before she went to St.
Mary's. Her father's liquor store was close to the Cleveland
theater, where James was playing leading roles. Actors were
in and out of the shop, and Thomas Quinlan got to know
his fellow-Irishman. There was a pleasant relationship between the businessmen of the town and its actors. Presently James was a familiar guest at Quinlan's home. Here
he was exposed to the adoring gaze of Ella, happy as any
teen-ager with her favorite star. No doubt she boasted to
her friends at St. Mary's. The association meant nothing to
James. Soon after she went to school, he left for Chicago.

They met again in New York in different circumstances. Ella had grown into a tallish girl of considerable
beauty with large brown eyes and a heavy knot of red-
brown hair. Her taste in dress, which was always exquisite,
lent her distinction. The Quinlans were well-to-do, and it
had been possible for Ella to make the most of her appearance in the ladies' stores for which New York was already
famous. Her father had died while she was at St. Mary's,
and she had persuaded her mother to bring her to New
York to go on with her musical education. What more
natural than that she should go backstage at the Union

Square Theater to claim acquaintance with her father's friend? Her early admiration was rapidly rekindled. At the height of his vigor and promise, surrounded by adoring fans, James was a young girl's dream. No doubt it seemed a miracle that he should love her. Even now, as we look back on the romance, it is his feeling and not Ella's which seems surprising.

Her superior social standing and education may have attracted him at the start. It would be unfair to suggest that he married Ella for mercenary motives, but it may well be that he was flattered by the attention of a girl of some wealth and refinement. Besides, hard-working and successful though he was, there was an emptiness in his personal life. Homeless, rootless, he had drifted apart from his family, which represented to him poverty and narrowness of outlook. He desperately needed a fixed and settled background, which the world of the theater could never provide him. In Ella he found a girl who had what he lacked. Innocent and convent-bred, she was different from the women he met in the course of his profession. Her music, too, set her apart from the common herd. James felt at once protective and dependent. He needed some sort of ideal to cling to. At the same time, he was anxious to shield her always from the roughness of life. Popular and self-assured, he thought he could.

Ella's mother was not so certain. Actors did not make good husbands. They never had homes of their own; they dragged their wives around on tour; they associated with other ladies professionally, sometimes with unfortunate results. They were not even good providers. As a rule they were irregularly paid, while their expenses in costumes and travel ran high. At the end of a season they were as often as not out of work, while the good times were seldom enough to pay for the bad ones. Ella had been brought up in comfort and was unused to money difficulties. She ought to make a better match. All her friends would think so. Thomas Quinlan, when he invited young O'Neill to his home, had never imagined for an instant that the actor would aspire to his own daughter.

All this and doubtless more Bridget Quinlan said to her daughter. She succeeded in postponing the match for a year and also in sowing the seeds of future trouble. Eventually, however, she was forced to give way. Ella was in love and mulishly obstinate. It is fair to say at this point that as far as love went, she was on firm ground. James had not reached thirty without some escapades in his past, but his future was devoted to Ella entirely. She gave him cause to be wearied with her later on, but he never was.

All might have been well if Ella had taken her mother's warnings in a constructive spirit. She had listened and even remembered, but she had not prepared herself to adapt to her husband's pattern. James, who adored her for her unworldly innocence, did nothing to help her. His professional life was lived entirely in public, and he thought of his wife less as a partner than as a sweet and private treasure of his own. It did not matter to him if she made few friends and saw few people. It was his privilege to protect her from the harsh world, which he did so thoroughly that business problems were all taken out of her hands. In fact, Ella soon became bored.

She was always conscious of having taken a step down, not so much in marrying James, who was of course going

24

to the top, as in associating with lesser actors and their wives. Some of these were undoubtedly a shady lot. Scandalous gossip, sometimes founded on fact, buzzed around the ladies of the cast. Their manners were freer than she was used to. Ella was naturally shy and shrank from their too-familiar advances.

She might have been content with a home of her own and quiet neighbors whom she could have got to know by slow degrees. Even this would have presented some difficulties, for her upbringing had been directed mainly to giving her social advantages. The Quinlans seem to have taken for granted her life would be easy. Accordingly Ella had been launched on matrimony without the smallest knowledge of how to keep a house. She could not cook and she could not train a servant. Perhaps this had not seemed to matter, since she must have known James lived in hotels. Probably she had no idea how grim these were in the provinces or what discomforts attended going on tour. Trains were dirty, small theaters dilapidated, cooking atrocious, restaurants few and far between. There was nothing to do on dreadful Sundays in strange towns. There was nowhere to be private except a series of impersonal bedrooms. There were no friends, only acquaintances, a fresh set to be made everywhere. Shy, fastidious Ella shrank from it all.

More distasteful perhaps than anything else was the whisky. How Ella ever married James without noticing the smell that hung about him remains a mystery. Not that James was a drunkard, either then or later in life. He merely got through a great deal of whisky during the day. Most of his fellow-actors did. It eased them over the strain of performances and the physical discomforts of their lives. Besides, they met in bars. Where else should they get together, having no homes?

No doubt Ella really made efforts to adapt herself to James, but her nature lacked resiliency. At all events she began, probably unconsciously, to store up a list of grievances which embittered the family life in years to come. She was really in love with James, however; and she never considered parting from him. For the moment, it no doubt seemed that difficulties were on their way to solution when young Jamie was born in 1878. Now Ella's life would have the interest which it had lacked.

Meanwhile, James' own career had run into trouble. He had attained the standing of a star and had considerable say in choosing his roles. His ambition, like that of the best actors he knew, was to star in Shakespeare; but for the present he hoped to build up his reputation by a series of popular successes. At this point surprisingly, his weaknesses showed.

James, as we have seen, was self-educated. As sometimes happens in such a case, he was deficient in taste. He understood Shakespeare because he had been constantly in the company of others who did. Impressed by the great performers, he had risen above the vulgar, ranting style of inferior actors. But when it came to choosing a play which would raise his reputation, his judgment was not sound. He opened in San Francisco as Jesus Christ in an ill-written Passion play which caused great scandal there. James had been quite serious, even to the extent of giving up drink and tobacco and conducting rehearsals in the solemn spirit of a church service. He had laid himself open, however, to the protests of those who saw the vulgarity of the production, as well as of those who objected to Christ being played on the stage. The enterprise was a failure. His next venture, though less notorious, was unsuccessful also. It looked as though he might be running into real trouble when Booth's Theater in New York offered him the star part in *The Count of Monte Cristo*.

The Count of Monte Cristo was a dramatization of Dumas's famous romance. Edmond Dantes, arrested secretly and imprisoned for life without trial on the accusation of a jealous rival, is befriended by a fellow-prisoner whose escape tunnel had accidentally led to his cell. The old man knows the secret of a vast hidden treasure, which he reveals to Dantes before he dies. Taking the place of the corpse, Dantes is thrown over the prison wall into the sea with a weight tied to his legs, this being the fashion in which the prison gets rid of its dead. Needless to say, he cuts himself loose, finds the treasure, and reappears in the world as the Count of Monte Cristo, rich, mysterious, and in search of revenge. His one-time fiancée has married his rival, and there are others who have played a part in getting Dantes out of the way. Cautiously the count introduces himself to them, part investigator, and part tempter. Eventually, in a dramatic fencing scene, he slays his enemies.

This fine old melodrama is not remarkable for consistency of plot, but it contains an agreeable mixture of costume, swordplay, romance, and adventure. Its special highpoint was the moment when the escaping Dantes crawled out of the stormy ocean waves, made of blue canvas and moving in realistic rolls behind him. Breathless he hauled himself up on a rock and, brandishing the dagger with which he had freed himself, cried out in tri-

umph, "The treasure of Monte Cristo! The world is mine!"
It brought down the house.

James O'Neill had everything this role required: the
looks, the swordplay, the splendid voice, the grace, the dramatic fire. He was a smashing success from the start. His
fortune was made.

It was made, but his career was ruined. Before he was
done with *Monte Cristo*, he was to climb that rock and cry,
"The world is mine!" six thousand times. Playing steadily
five nights a week, six thousand performances would have
taken about twenty-four years. Actually James made some
efforts to get free from his slavery, but in vain. He *was*
Edmond Dantes to a generation of American theatergoers.
The public would not see him as anything else.

It is easy to imagine James riding the crest of exhilaration at the time of his first, unbelievable hit; next consent-
ing to prolong his role; then becoming bored with it; de-
scending finally to such an extreme of nausea that he
could hardly keep his mind on the familiar lines. To be
sure, he enjoyed the applause. But he had aspired to
greater things than climbing that rock. He looked for ways
out, but never found any. He needed the money.

This may seem extraordinary in view of the fact that
James made eight hundred thousand dollars out of the
play in twenty-five years at a period when there was no
income tax and when money was several times as valuable
as it is at present. He ought to have been a rich man.
Indeed, in a way he was, yet he had two weaknesses. They
both stemmed probably from those bad times of his boy-
hood, and both were facets of the same thing: he was
irrationally anxious about money. On the one hand, he

always thought he was going to end up in the poorhouse. No amount of savings ever meant that he felt safe. On the other hand, and for the very same reason, he was a natural mark for every confidence trickster who had a get-rich scheme to sell. James grabbed at any fraudulent mine puffed up by a fancy prospectus. He also had a weakness for the possession of land, inherited doubtless from his Irish peasant background, which made him the ideal sucker for dubious operations in real estate. Such mistakes kept his fortune within bounds. Anxiety did the rest. It was soon aggravated by the weight of wife and sons, dependent on him.

Ella had made a too affectionate mother. Hers was the intense love which does damage, being less concerned with giving than with getting a response. When little Jamie was four, she had a second son, Edmund. It became obvious that she could no longer, at least for a time, take the children on circuit with her husband. Jamie had been bedded down in bureau drawers and nursed somehow through eight-hour train journeys with no restaurant car. Two small children could not possibly be fitted into a traveling life. James bought a house in New London, Connecticut, where Ella had family connections. A summer resort and not too far from New York, New London was to serve the family as their nearest thing to a permanent home for many years. Presently, however, Ella's love for her husband prevailed over her maternal instincts. He needed her; and she joined him, leaving the children with her mother. She soon had word that Jamie was down with measles. Little Edmund, not yet a year and a half old, caught the disease and died.

Ella could not get over the tragedy. She blamed herself for leaving the child and, to suppress such feelings, blamed her husband and even young Jamie. She conceived the notion that Jamie had been jealous of the new baby and had deliberately exposed his brother to measles in hopes that he would die. This gave her, perhaps, an excuse for what must now be done. They packed Jamie off to a boarding school at seven years old, and Ella resumed the circuit with her husband.

Ella's view of her duty to her husband was simple and old-fashioned, like her religion and no doubt James had been insistent that she travel with him. There was a hard and selfish core in James. But Ella, maternal enough to be torn, was not strong enough to stand the strain of conflicting feelings. She blamed her husband and her son alternately, never herself. Nor did she desire another child to pain her in the same way. When, three years later, she found she was pregnant again, she felt despairing. James, as usual, was on tour to packed houses. He could not disappoint his public, and she could not be with him. She remained in New York. It was in New York, then, in a private hotel where the family stayed while in town, that Eugene Gladstone O'Neill was born in 1888, child of a reluctant mother and a father too busy to spend more than four days waiting for his birth.

He was a healthy child, but his mother had a hard time. She was attended by a doctor whom James had met casually in a barroom. It is fair to say that most of James's acquaintances were made in this fashion. He was a healthy man and probably had little knowledge of doctors. It may have been true. as Eugene later said, that he was happy to get these services cheap. To acquaintances, James was the most generous of men. Toward his family he was often mean. His obsession with money led him to cut corners in peculiar ways. It was this doctor who, when Ella complained of pain, prescribed morphine.

Morphine is a dangerous drug, though it is by no means usual for a person to become addicted readily. It acts as a tranquilizer, blurring problems and making reality seem a distant dream. For those who are not strong enough to endure the conditions under which they happen to be living, it offers escape. It did this now for Ella. She had already proved herself unable to face the very real troubles of her life. She took to the drug. James, unsuspicious and aware that childbirth had mysterious aftereffects, was not enlightened till too late. Cures proved no more than temporary. From this time onward, Ella could not be counted on. She retreated into a dreamworld of her own in which, if *A Long Day's Journey Into Night* is to be believed, she played remorselessly on the emotions of her husband and sons. James had dragged her down. He had diverted her attention from God's call to be a nun. He had ruined her career as a musician. All her friends had cast her off for marrying an actor. She loved him, of course; but he had given her nothing, not even a home. Her life had been tragedy. Jamie had murdered his little brother by giving him the measles. Eugene by his very birth had caused his mother's illness.

In a situation of this kind, it was hardly possible that Eugene's childhood should have been a happy one. For the first seven years of his life he traveled with his parents and his nanny, Sarah Shandy, who made up for the deficiencies of Ella. The conditions of James O'Neill's life had not improved with the continuing success of *Monte Cristo*. It took him permanently out of repertory and sent him on tour throughout the theatrical season, frequently to one-night stops. To be sure, Ella and the baby were spared the daily moves by being sent ahead to places where James might spend a few days, or even a week. But the ceaseless succession of railroad trips and poor hotels continued for nine months of the year. There was no home life except in New London. They never stayed anywhere long enough for a little boy to find a playmate.

Sarah Shandy was the warmest part of this impersonal existence. She really loved Eugene and took some trouble to find outings suitable for a little boy, to zoos or circuses, in compensation for his lack of friends. But Sarah was a frustrated woman, and possibly she found the theatrical circuit as dreary as Ella and Eugene did. At all events, she craved vicarious excitement and had a passion for lurid murders and horror tales, which she shared with Eugene. The effect of these on a sensitive little boy with no other companion may be imagined. Eugene never complained of Sarah later on. He never suggested that she had played any part in distorting his life. But he mentioned having continual nightmares when he was little. His own imagination, growing with what it fed on, became in later life as lurid as Sarah's.

Home was some hotel or other. The nursery was backstage. He saw *Monte Cristo*, as it were, from behind. "Dripping with salt and sawdust," James climbed painfully onto a stool behind the swinging canvas waves to cry, "The world is mine!" The spotlight focused on him, and the audience burst into frantic applause. There was no glamor in it from the wings. The illusion was not created for Eugene, and repetition dulled any effect it might have had. Even Sarah got to know the play so well that she claimed she could have taken any part at a moment's notice.

Summer meant New London. There was a certain stability in this, but Eugene still did not find many playmates. He had inherited, it soon turned out, Ella's unfortunate shyness. Besides, a boy who leads a solitary life for most of the year can hardly be expected to become suddenly outgoing. There were cousins in New London whom he saw occasionally. The relationship, however, was never truly cordial because Ella kept apart from her relatives.

Torn between her love for her boys and for her husband, Ella had retreated with the aid of her drug from the whole problem. Her affection was tantalizingly unsteady. She demanded and she promised, but she did not satisfy. Every so often she would go away for a mysterious "cure" which was not explained to Eugene.

Small wonder that, as soon as he was old enough, Eugene's nose was generally in a book. Like his mother, he was learning to escape. When he was not reading, he seemed to be simply brooding much of the time. A photograph taken when he was seven shows him as a thin figure in long, dark stockings and short pants with a schoolboy cap on his head. He is sitting alone on a rock and staring out to sea with an expression of melancholy which is pathetic for a boy of his age. His relations considered him delicate, which he was not. His father and mother, immersed in their own concerns, did not seem to notice that he was troubled.

3   A MIXED-UP BOY

James o'neill was not an understanding father, but his intentions were generally good. He had learned the hard way that an education is of inestimable value, and he intended to see that his sons had every advantage. He picked out, therefore, an excellent Catholic boarding school in the Bronx called Mount Saint Vincent, where Eugene was sent shortly before his seventh birthday.

It is difficult to see what else James could have done.

The lonely, rootless life of theatrical touring was unsuitable, both for education and for mixing with other boys. Ella's drug habit was a problem of such enormous dimensions that James must have felt relief at getting a pair of inquisitive eyes out of the way. Mount Saint Vincent was a small school run by Sisters of Charity, who also kept a larger school for girls. There were only fifteen boys between seven and twelve. They lived and studied in a cottage nearly a mile from the main building in a corner of a fifty-five-acre estate which had once belonged to the actor Edwin Forrest. The boys came from good families. The curriculum was sensible. There was plenty of free time. But the arrangement did not suit Eugene.

It meant in the first place separation from Sarah, who left to take another job. It meant losing a family life to which he clung with desperation, precisely because there was too little of it. That summer in New London he had acquired a dog, no doubt on the understanding that it would have to be left behind. The parting, however, was an additional blow. After much pleading, he got permission to have the animal at Mount Saint Vincent. He wrote for it. The letter arrived one day after the dog had been run over and killed.

A thicker-skinned boy would have got over these troubles in time and made the friends he really needed. Eugene did not. He went through agonies of loneliness after every vacation, suffering the pangs of parting from home all over again. He was not unpopular with the boys, but he did not say much, even to his roommate. He read more advanced books than the others, and he cared little for their sports. School was something imposed on him by grownups against his will, and he held himself apart.

Religion, of course, was an integral part of the curriculum. Ella's devoutness had waned somewhat under the influence of her drug, but fundamentally the Catholic faith was always vital to her. Ella was sentimental and kind, and it seems that Eugene's attention had not been directed to the sterner side of his religion, to the doctrines of purgatory and punishment. They shocked him. He accepted them, as a child will, and went through the early stages of Catholic training without serious question. But the experience left a mark. Moreover, family troubles were on the increase, and somehow religion did not provide a way to cope with them.

The older Eugene grew, the more obvious it was becoming that something or other was seriously wrong with his mother. This in itself was bad enough, but it at least was no new problem. Eugene was only ten years of age when it began to be evident that something was also wrong with his brother Jamie.

Jamie had been an attractive boy, more so indeed than Eugene, since he had inherited a good deal of his father's gregarious charm. But he likewise had suffered from lack of a home and want of understanding. The brothers, considering their ten years' difference in age, were exceedingly close. Eugene adored Jamie, as a little boy often will his older brother. Jamie was the only person in the world who really understood his unhappiness because Jamie shared it. Unfortunately, Jamie felt the bond also. He chose Eugene to confide in, and Jamie was going through a difficult stage.

While Eugene was going to Mount Saint Vincent, Jamie graduated from a Catholic preparatory school and moved on to a Catholic college, both in New York. But already before leaving school he had made experiments in drink and dissipation. He was utterly cynical about religion and about life, confiding his feelings to Eugene, who was too young to cope with them. By the time he was twenty, Jamie was already an alcoholic. The dimensions of his problem were by no means obvious yet, but he was the worst possible influence on a ten-year-old boy. Eugene, wavering betwen religion and despair, became more devout. Privately he was making a bargain with God. If devotion would not help his family problems, what use was religion?

Eugene grew out of Mount Saint Vincent when he was twelve years old. At last the pattern of boarding school and loneliness was to be broken. He was sent to De La Salle, run by the Christian Brothers in Manhattan. He was to live at home with Ella, who was established for the purpose in a hotel on Sixty-eighth Street, a few blocks from the school.

Presumably this had been Ella's idea and may have represented a real effort to give Eugene what she must at times have known he needed. If so, her good resolutions did not last. Eugene, returning unexpectedly one day, disturbed his mother in the act of giving herself a morphine injection. He would not have understood what this meant, but Ella was in no condition to keep her head. Hysterically she accused him of spying on her. Naturally it followed that James and Jamie had to explain what was really the matter.

Eugene understood at last. It was actually a relief. Ella's addiction provided a reason, external to himself, for everything which went wrong. It also gave him something to ask God for, a definite challenge which he could present to his religion. He would devote himself to piety and good works if God would cure his mother.

Eugene gave faith what seemed a fair trial. He was sent to board at De La Salle, and his resolutions lasted through the rest of this year and most of another. But at the age of fourteen, when Ella was no better, he told his parents he was through with Catholic schools. Religion, he said resentfully, had been no use to them. Why force it on him? James and Ella reluctantly gave way. Eugene entered Betts Academy in Stamford, Connecticut, a nonsectarian school. The following summer, on a Sunday morning in New London, he met his father coming downstairs for church and told him that he was never going to church again.

There was an actual struggle on the stairs. James shouted and tried to shake sense into Eugene. The boy twisted and pulled to get away. Somehow they got to the bottom of the stairs without falling and glared at each other in fury and defiance. There was nothing James could really do. He could not drag Eugene through the streets of New London. He stamped off alone. Eugene was left with a victory which he only half wanted and in a sense regretted all his life.

Betts was a school of about sixty boys with high academic standards, good athletics, and reasonable discipline. Eugene did better at Betts and liked it more than he had his other schools. He made friends, began uncertainly to show an interest in girls. He still did not bother about athletics, and he had a normal pleasure in taking the risks involved in breaking rules. But he and the school found each other satisfactory. Presumably the masters knew that he took friends to New York some weekends in order to see current plays, to which as an actor's son he got free tickets. There was no harm in that. If they also found out that his friends thought that he was worldly-wise, they would have imagined he had done some showing off. The truth was far different. Eugene was concealing, not displaying his sophistication.

Jamie had been thrown out of college. His father insisted that he adopt some profession. Jamie took the easiest course, a minor role in *Monte Cristo*. James beamed with pride over his debut, and Jamie had inherited his fine voice and some of his looks. But he did not care about acting or want to work. Nor did he have any feeling for his father which might have induced him not to shame the old man publicly. On the contrary, he loathed James, whom he had always considered as a rival for the affections of his mother. Besides, he had grown up with *Monte Cristo* and had no illusions about its merits. Ever since his childhood, the old man had been making a fool of himself in that ranting piece. Jamie's feelings toward his father were a queer mixture of embarrassment and resentment.

For both their sakes he should have struck out for

himself. To do so, however, meant work, meant facing criticism from people who would employ him on his merits. Jamie, who was already drinking hard, scarcely attempted independence. He stayed on with the old man, loathing him, the play, and intermittently himself. Before long, no one else would hire him. He had not merely ceased to bother about his role. He took actual pleasure in muffing his lines, coming drunk on-stage, and creating scandals which it took all the old man's seasoned skill to cover up.

James did not turn him out. His home, his acting company were open to Jamie, no matter how badly he behaved. Yet Jamie gave him no credit for this. Gene, who was ten years younger, followed Jamie's lead. In fact, Gene adored Jamie and sided with his mother, while resenting and even hating his father. This may seem strange, considering James's undoubted virtues, but so it was. Patiently devoted to Ella through years of the most trying illness, tolerant of Jamie under great provocation, tied for twenty-five years to that ridiculous play in part for his family's sake, James was regarded by both his sons as the villain of the piece.

The truth seems to have been that he was difficult to live with. Friends saw him as generous and jolly. To his sons, he seemed a miser and a bully. Love of applause was in his make-up. It had led him to take up an acting career. It had deluded him with the initial success of *Monte Cristo*. He always wanted the leading role and, part unconsciously, humiliated his sons. Where Ella indulged them, he criticized. Where she praised them, he jeered. The boys had become his rivals for his wife's attention, and he was jealous of them. His very energies were against him. He could never let a subject go or a conflict rest. He had to assert himself not once in a while, but all the time.

The resentment of his sons grew and found plenty to feed on. James was mean in little ways. Ella complained he had found her a cheap doctor. Gene represents him economizing absurdly over light bulbs or cutting his own hedge at a time when nobody of his standing in New London would think of doing such a thing. He had an admiration for low cunning and cheap tricks. When Jamie tried to pick the lock of the whisky cupboard and failed, his father was not angry or despairing. He was elated. He had got the better of Jamie and had noticed the scratches on the lock. He was too busy gloating to be helpful. One is tempted to wonder whether he did not in a way enjoy the atmosphere of his home. One thing is certain. His younger son hated it.

Underneath, Eugene was miserable as ever, perhaps more so. Adolescence is always a difficult time, and the peculiarities of his family grated on him daily. Even in New London he felt out of place. His father was more at home in a hotel bar than in a summer resort. His mother, retreating into her dream world, kept at a distance even her aunt and cousins, who, though living in New London, hardly knew her. Meanwhile, the town was becoming fashionable. Shy boys who feel insecure are always anxious to merge into the scenery. There was nothing fashionable about the O'Neills' house, which was invincibly middle-class. This might have mattered less had not Ella drawn the family's attention to it by harping on the subject.

James, who was more unself-conscious, stuck stoutly to the kind of living he preferred. All in all, there was still little for young Eugene to cling to except Jamie. It is flattering for a boy to be taken up by his big brother.

In this way an alliance was being formed which might well have been Eugene's ruin. Jamie was still at the height of what might be called his career. Drink and dissipation had not lost their savor yet. They were less a compulsion than an exciting part of his war on his father. Jamie began to take Eugene about at weekends or in school holidays, exposing him to scenes and habits which he might in decency have spared so young a boy. The brothers had in common a wild gaiety when excited. Gene entered into episodes which gave him afterward an uneasy sense of guilt, despite the cynicism which his brother was teaching. Such experiences set him apart from his schoolmates, made him more dependent on Jamie, and deepened his obsession with family problems. Later evidence suggests that whenever Gene and Jamie got together, their talk degenerated into mocking stories about their old man and *Monte Cristo*.

Such was the background of the quiet, well-mannered boy of seventeen who graduated from Betts Academy in 1906. He had not the reputation among his friends of being miserable. On the contrary, some envied him his famous, jolly father, the family motorcar, a rare luxury in those days, his own boat in New London. It is true that he was always short of cash. Considering Jamie's tuition and the use Eugene made of what money he got, it seems possible that James was justified in drawing the purse strings tight. Gene put it down to meanness. He especially resented having to earn money by helping his father clip the hedge. It made him conspicuous.

Betts was a preparatory school for Yale. All his friends were going there, so that he made up his mind he would go to Princeton. It was a small gesture of defiance. James insisted on college. Eugene wanted no sort of continuation of school, but he had no alternative to propose. He would certainly not join his father and brother. He hated acting.

He disliked Princeton at once. Princeton had its clubs and traditions. Eugene was not good club material, while New London had taught him to resent the slightest suspicion of snobbish exclusiveness. He had no school spirit either. Classes bored him. He resented being told to appreciate Ibsen, whom he had discovered for himself. But he equally disliked the study of Shakespeare because he had not learned to enjoy him yet and did not intend to except in his own good time. On the basis of his freshman studies he decided that Princeton was not intellectually stimulating. It was not in touch with real problems. Eugene proceeded to tackle these in dives in Trenton or with the help of bottles in his room. On the whole his contemporaries did not think much of him. A few friends penetrated his protective shell and found him charming.

The following June he got himself suspended for throwing stones, climbing onto a porch, and kicking furniture over, as he walked home with a couple of friends after a rowdy party in Trenton. Since he had also cut his final exams, he was soon dropped by the college and returned to his father as a failure.

James, since this was his way, surely consoled himself by exclaiming, "I told you so!" or "Just like Jamie!" and "Neither of the boys is any good!" He wanted Eugene to prove himself, and these were his methods of trying to force a contradiction out of his son.

In this he failed. Gene made little effort to justify himself. In fact, while Jamie had at least condescended to adopt a career, Gene seemed to prefer doing nothing. He lived with his parents for a while, failed at a secretarial job which James got for him, and argued his father out of a few months' support while he looked around him. Thereupon he moved out of free quarters in his parents' hotel to share an apartment with a couple of struggling artists on Sixty-sixth Street.

They at least were trying to paint. Gene was chiefly hanging about the Unique Bookshop, kept by an anarchist and left-wing agitator of considerable note. Gene had discovered the writings of Nietzsche and was enthralled by his wholesale rejection of the Christian virtues of humility, poverty, acceptance of being or having less than the best. The Catholicism which still attracted and repelled him seemed to roll off his shoulders like a weight. But Nietzsche proved a more destructive than positive force. Turning his back on his parents' faith, Eugene pressed forward, he never quite knew whither. Every so often in later life he appeared to be working out a solution in which his ancient faith and new convictions reached some harmony. He never succeeded, and the pessimism of his last plays becomes blacker because he is resigned to not finding much meaning behind the drama of life. *The Iceman Cometh*

44

is a monument to the failure of a quest which had started in an anarchist bookshop on Sixth Avenue before Gene was twenty years old.

Had his father but known it, he was continuing his education after a fashion which made sense to him. Such an activity marked him out for a future very different from Jamie's. At the moment, however, there seemed little to choose between them. Gene was drinking. He was behaving as wildly as his brother and collecting these impious ideas as well. His friends were bohemian. Louis Halliday, an exuberant young man who was his greatest friend at this period, was a brother of Polly Halliday, whose restaurant was a center of Greenwich Village artistic life. Louis drank a good deal, and his circle must have seemed disreputable to James, whose ideas and standards were old-fashioned.

Presently Eugene gave another sign of being less fitted to handle a dissipated life than his brother was. As usual, it was the sort of sign which made his father take a darker view. He got himself involved with a girl.

She was Kathleen Jenkins, blond and pretty, of conventional background, a typical nice girl. She was perhaps a little bored. There was not much occupation for a girl over eighteen those days except parties and meeting young men. Since one moved in a limited circle, young men tended to be cut after the same pattern. Eugene was different. Handsome, shy, intense, and gloomy-looking, he fascinated Kathleen. He was worldly yet naïve, soft yet hard. The truth was, she had penetrated his armor. Nice girls were something new in Eugene's personal life. He talked to her about his ideas. She was not a Catholic to be shocked by his loss of faith, while her mental horizons were ready for enlargement.

They were soon in love. What he had not reckoned on was that Kathleen meant marriage. Why not? She had been brought up for marriage and had been given no other purpose in life since she left school. They loved each other. Gene had no profession; but his father must be quite well-to-do, while Kathleen's family was not poor. She had not much worldly knowledge, and the thing seemed simple to her.

It was far from so to Eugene. Inside himself, he was all at sixes and sevens. The last thing that he wanted was responsibility. He would have to conform, become what others considered a decent member of society. Society! His friend in the anarchist bookshop had shown him that his hatred for everything that had happened to him was not primarily a grudge against his father. Why, the old man and he himself were victims of society! It was the outside pressures of the world on an individual which destroyed him.

He actually appealed to his father for help. He was well aware that James would not permit him to get married at twenty to a non-Catholic girl and without any prospect of being able to support a family. James rushed into the breach with characteristic energy. His own obsessions warned him that the Jenkinses were after his money. They thought him a rich man! Of course they did! They had deliberately trapped his son! It took James little time to arrange a trip to Spanish Honduras for Eugene. An acquaintance of his was going out there to look into the prospects of a gold mine in which James had persuaded Ella to invest.

It soon appeared that James had overreached himself. His assumption that Kathleen and the Jenkinses were quite unscrupulous had increased Eugene's distress, since he knew they were not. He felt more obligated to Kathleen than ever. In any case, he was going to Honduras and would not have to face responsibility for quite some time. He was very much his mother's son, and he did not think about an uncomfortable future. He merely gave in on both sides to pressures now. He slipped away secretly to marry Kathleen; then he sailed for Honduras.

As a solution to his problems, the trip was useless. He hated Honduras, its natives, its food, its endless insect life. The gold they had come to look for did not exist. He got malaria. After six and a half months, he was home again. Kathleen had written that since she was going to have a baby, he would have to admit the marriage to his father. He had done so. James was furious, and Gene himself was appalled. He could not think why he had been such a fool, and he never wanted to see Kathleen again.

While he wondered what on earth to do, his son was born. Kathleen's mother understandably lost patience with the O'Neills. She revealed the marriage and birth to the newspapers, adding that her son-in-law was at present in Honduras. Gene learned of his fatherhood in a New York bar when the barman handed him a copy of the paper. Mrs. Jenkins learned from the press a few days later that the missing husband had been in town at least a week!

James, still refusing to recognize the facts, whisked

his son off on tour as assistant manager. Gene went, hating the work and, doubtless, himself. His father had convinced him that he had been unfairly trapped. James held the purse strings and would not finance the marriage. He himself neither wanted nor was able to support Kathleen. He did not go to see her because there was no use in it. He had long ceased to regard her as anything but a millstone about his neck. His feelings toward the unwanted baby were not paternal.

He had to get away. His growing misery made everything ahead unbearable. He made the sort of break that many another has done in revolt against hard realities. He went to sea.

4   A YOUNG MAN IN SEARCH
OF HIMSELF

IT WAS 1910. James O'Neill was playing in Boston, and his son had taken to hanging about the docks and talking to seamen. These were the last days of sailing ships, but romance still lingered about a port. Eugene had watched ships go out from New London. He had himself sailed from San Francisco to Honduras. He was reading the greatest of Conrad's tales of the sea. As in Conrad's case, the rhythm, the beauty, the vastness of the sea made an irresistible appeal to his nature. Some feel this sea-longing, while others do not understand it. With a few, it can grow into a passion. It was so with young O'Neill.

On the one side was the acting trade he loathed, the marriage he felt had been forced on him, the society with which he was at odds. On the other was the lure of the sea itself, coupled with a challenge to prove his worth in physical terms. Eugene signed up on the *Charles Racine*, a Norwegian square-rigger, one of the last. She was taking lumber to Buenos Aires and carried a crew of thirty-five. Surprisingly, James O'Neill approved the step. He thought the experience might pull his son together.

For the first time in Eugene's life everything went right for him. Seafaring was exciting. There was the thrill of reefing sail a hundred and fifty feet above deck, the ecstasy of watching the dawn come up, the challenge of toiling sixteen hours at a stretch in dirty weather. Even the dull jobs like holystoning the deck were of a nature which deadened anxious thoughts. In those days before wireless was general, one had the sense of being in a little world of one's own for the length of a voyage, a wonderful relief for a boy whose unsolved problems had driven him to flight.

More surprisingly, he liked the men. His awkward shyness had always made people a difficulty to him. He had never fitted into a group before, and the experience was a revelation. The merchant seamen of the *Charles Racine* were simple fellows without a general idea in their heads. They had, however, a wealth of experiences, dangerous or lurid, gained from knocking about all over the world. They were used to the cramped quarters of the fo'c'sle, where it is necessary to live and let live. They accepted Eugene without question, only demanding that he do his fair share of work and obey their rules.

With an extraordinary sense of relief, he found the conditions of this new life acceptable. Irritated by his father, egged on by Jamie, resentful of school or college, he had come perilously close to defying all rules. On shipboard, they became tolerable. Life in the fo'c'sle would be impossible unless each let the others' possessions alone. The ship was their world, and, therefore, devotion to her must come first. Sails must be taken in or spread, rope must be spliced, no matter what the danger. It was even obvious that crowded quarters must be kept spotlessly clean. Here, in this little pocket of existence, stripped down to a simple level, Eugene was not at war with his society. He belonged at last.

Perhaps this experience was summed up for him by the chanteys. The hauling, all together, as someone gave the timing with one of those swinging songs meant something he never forgot. He never cared much about more complex music and had no sort of a voice, but the sound of the chanteys stayed with him all his life and crept into his plays. "Shenandoah," for instance, opens his mighty tragedy, *Mourning Becomes Electra*.

To be sure, a seaman's life is not comfortable. The food was horrible, worse than that in Honduras. Indeed, it mainly consisted of salt pork, pea soup, and hardtack which had to be broken with a marlin spike and tapped on the table to knock out the worms. Quarters were crowded. If his new friends took him without question, he was too imaginative to do so in return. He says of himself in a poem afterward that he loved all the drawbacks of the life as well as its pleasures. They were part of the game. But he did not ship out again from Buenos Aires. Perhaps the trouble was that to him it really had been a game. He had spent sixty-five days out of sight of land in a special world of its own. But he did not belong there, and he dared not go back to face realities.

Perhaps his reasons were more casual. Swaggering ashore like a seasoned sailor, he spent all his pay in a waterfront dive on the first night. Then he got a series of jobs, quitting each to squander his money in the same way as before. He struck up a friendship with a young Englishman who had gone to the dogs and was trying to pull himself together. Presently he saw that he himself was getting nowhere, and he signed on a cattle boat that was going to Durban.

Seagoing was a different experience this time. He never spoke very freely about this trip, but he disliked it. Maybe he simply did not care for tending cattle. At all events, to his disappointment he was not allowed to go ashore in Durban because he could not put down a hundred dollars. There was nothing for it but to go back with the ship to Buenos Aires.

This time he really hit bottom. His sense of discovering himself may have been blunted by his cattle-boat adventure. At all events, his reaction now was to try the kind of freedom which comes from being too low to fall anywhere. He slept on park benches, dodging the police; or he shared with friends crude shelters put together out of materials which had been scavenged from the refuse of the waterfront. He begged for food, or better still cheap liquor. He followed a down-and-out sailor's custom by dangling an old tin can on a rope outside the cook's galley of any ship which happened to be in port. Yet in spite of it all, his mind was at work. He was observing life around him, and it had even occurred to him he might want to write some day. He was on the way to becoming a hopeless drunk, but a sense of self-preservation did remain. Eventually he faced the fact he had to get out of Buenos Aires; and he shipped on the S.S. *Ikalis*, bound for New York. He must have known that he would have to take up the life he had abandoned, and the last months may have been consumed in getting up his courage.

The *Ikalis* was a British tramp steamer with a crew of thirty. Compared to the *Charles Racine* she was not romantic. Work for the inexperienced was mostly scrubbing and painting. The crew was the usual mixture of odds and ends. The *Ikalis* was a casual laborer of the sea, going where her cargo took her. She was not the ship for settled, married seamen, who wanted a home port and regular run. Eugene liked the crew, divided this time into stokers, A.B.s, and ordinary seamen. Some of them were to appear in his plays, as did the *Ikalis* under the name S.S. *Glencairn*. He studied the A.B.s' tasks, eager for promotion from duller, harder jobs. The voyage, however, took only a month, and he had no present intention of shipping out of New York.

Surprisingly at first sight, he did not go back to his parents. He plunged instead into another episode which reminds one of the months in Buenos Aires. Again it seems that he was getting up his courage.

He paid three dollars for a month's rent at a rooming house called Jimmy-the-Priest's down near the docks. This was a filthy, bug-infested place where people who could not afford any lodging might sleep in the back room with their heads on the table if they bought a nickel's worth of beer or whisky. Eugene had one of two beds in a tiny room looking out on a fire escape. He spent his days drinking, or lounging in Battery Park. For the most part, he lived off the free soup which Jimmy's served to the roomers at noon. But he was not happy.

He must either go home or get work, and both were distasteful. He had been away for a year and had nothing to show, save the habit of drinking. It was getting a hold on him, and to go to sea meant giving up whisky. Besides, seafaring was all very well as an adventure, but he had to reach desperation before he could face it. It involved too radical a change and demanded too much. A down-and-outer's life faced no demands. Presently, he pulled himself together, wrote to James announcing his arrival, and asked for money. James sent him some, on condition he use it for coming home. He spent it on drink, getting up his courage. When he recovered, he thought it better not to apply to James for more.

He had to go to sea or starve. He signed on the *S.S. New York*, one of the earliest luxury liners on the transatlantic run. He was accepted as an A.B. and went aboard proudly, only to be disillusioned in short order. Living conditions on the *S.S. New York* were better than on the tramp cargo ships he had previously worked on. But he found himself handling a mop and a bucket, just as though he had not been an A.B. What was worse, the passengers condescended to him, or else he thought they did. He was fiercely resentful. This experience made the trip a lark no more, but a degradation. He was glad to get off the *New York* at Liverpool, but he did not want to stay in England. He soon signed up on the *Philadelphia*, sister ship to the *New York*. He might find the liners unpleasant, but they were the quickest way of crossing the Atlantic. In New York he drew his pay and headed back to Jimmy-the-Priest's.

Life simplified itself again into keeping going at Jimmy's. He seemed a hopeless drunk, and yet he took the trouble to make trips uptown to watch the Irish Players from the Abbey Theatre in Dublin, who were soon also to stir Jig Cook in Chicago and lead to a meeting in Provincetown in 1916.

He was existing in this way when his past caught up with him. Kathleen Jenkins was seeking a divorce. She would take her son and get out of his life without asking a penny if Eugene would cooperate by providing proof of his dissolute habits.

He did so, but his self-loathing grew unbearable. What had he done for poor Kathleen but run away? If his father's suspicions of her had found any root in his own mind, they must have been banished now. She asked nothing but freedom. Disgust brought him partly to his senses. He knew perfectly well where James was playing, though he pretended he was cut off from his family.

Gambling in hopes of raising some cash, he had a lucky break. A few days later he was on his way to New Orleans, where *Monte Cristo* was about to open.

James was ready to welcome him, but he would not accept a grown son as a pensioner. He put Eugene on the payroll as Dantes's jailor, silencing his protests with the retort that he would only have one line to utter.

Poor James was near the end of his long role. The theaters had had enough of *Monte Cristo* after over twenty-five years, and its aging principal was in his mid-sixties. Someone had put together a dreadful cut-down version which took forty-five minutes. It appeared on a vaudeville bill, together with a trained-horse act and some flying acrobats. Jamie was playing one of the villains. What James thought and said when he had to cover up for two sons, both constantly drunk, may be imagined.

Jamie and Eugene were behaving worse than ever. They were humiliated by the horrible show, and each played on the other's resentment. The old man, they complained, did not need the money. This ghastly production, which was making a public spectacle of them all, had been undertaken by James out of nothing but avarice. Eventually their conduct forced their father to cancel his contract while it still had months to run. Ella was in a sanitarium undergoing a cure. Eugene headed back to Jimmy-the-Priest's to forget his family.

This recurring urge to drown his sorrows in whisky was beginning, perhaps, to lose appeal. It solved no problems, unless he drank himself to death. He brooded over death. Eventually, when James was back in New York and would be sure to hear of the incident, Eugene swallowed sleeping pills. Whether his life was saved by his friends or whether the action was little more than a gesture remains uncertain. Whatever happened, the episode clarified one thing in his mind. He wanted to live.

Life soon offered hope once more. Ella had completed her cure. As always, her husband looked on it as a permanent one. James had been appalled by the suicide attempt and was now ready to take into account what Eugene wanted. They made an arrangement that he should come to New London for the summer, and that James should get him a job on the local paper.

The *New London Telegraph* was a daily paper and a good one. It covered national news, but employed a few reporters locally. Eugene fitted pretty well into this casual group. He even attracted attention from the proprietor, an old friend of James's, who was astounded by Eugene's imaginative sympathies and deep feelings. The editor who supervised his copy was less impressed. Eugene was still a square peg in a round hole. He did not like news-gathering and did it badly. His shyness was a great drawback, while his lack of interest in detail was profound. He did make a name for himself on the editorial page with humorous, sometimes witty verse on topical subjects. Perhaps for this reason, perhaps because, as it was whispered, James paid his salary, he lasted till mid-October, when he caught a cold.

At first there was not much alarm. James was away making a motion-picture version of *Monte Cristo*. Jamie was taking a cure. Ella was passive and hardly even keeping house. Even Eugene's meals had to be brought in from outside. Presently pleurisy was diagnosed, and, after that, tuberculosis. Eugene always thought he picked up the infection from some of his fellow-roomers at Jimmy-the-Priest's.

James was feeling particularly poor. He was worth over a hundred thousand dollars; but much was unwisely invested, and he could not readily lay hands on it. Another company had come out with a film on *Monte Cristo*, and James's had to be withdrawn. He had accepted a role in a Broadway play, but plays were failures as often as they were hits. By now no optimist could imagine that Jamie would support himself. Eugene, who had seemed for a while to promise better, had broken down in health. Tuberculosis, scourge of the slums where he had grown up, may have appeared to James a death sentence. It was certainly the greatest killer in the country at that time. Thus, finding himself burdened with wife and elder son, his prospects failing, and the shadow of that dreaded poorhouse falling gloomily across his path, James seems to have decided to keep what he had for those most likely to live. He made arrangements to send Eugene to a state sanitarium, where the fee would be only four dollars a week. Irrationally, but characteristically, he called in a good tailor to make Eugene a suit before he went.

If *A Long Day's Journey Into Night* is to be believed, this latest vagary of James's was the thing about his father which Eugene found hardest to forgive. One must sympathize with him. The sanitarium was nothing but an old farmhouse flanked by a row of wooden shacks. The inhabitants were mostly very ill, and the atmosphere was one of hopelessness. The doctor was an intelligent man who perceived that Eugene, whose case was a light one, both needed and could pay for better treatment. He advised Gaylord Farm in Wallingford.

Eugene left for New York to argue with his father in what one may presume were bitter tones. Such scenes are never readily forgotten. James, whose intentions were always better than his judgment, was shamed into doing what he should have done all along. To Gaylord Farm Eugene went.

In six months he was discharged, cured not merely of a light bout of tuberculosis. Gaylord Sanitarium had given him a chance to think. Hitherto he had been battling either with his father or with the hardships of a seaman's life, or he had been drowning thought entirely. The cure at Gaylord was compounded of rest, good food, fresh air. His fellow-patients were not drifters. They were making a fight for life, as he himself was forced to do. There was no room for self-pity. Many stories could compare for tragedy with his own. Gaylord Sanitarium concerned itself with living, rather than dying. In its atmosphere, a sensitive young man began to take stock.

He had already considered that he might write plays. He had been more or less brought up in the theater. He knew its physical conditions and the technical limitations it imposes on the playwright. He knew it from the actor's point of view, from the manager's. The only side of it for which he retained nothing but contempt was the box office. It never occurred to him to write for popular success. Either the public would meet him on his own terms or not at all.

He returned to New London with a trivial one-act melodrama in his luggage and a number of incomplete ideas. He had been told to take things easy, and he did so. The O'Neill family was going through one of its better periods. James had been playing both Jacob and Pharaoh in a Broadway spectacle called *Joseph and His Brethren* which was going on tour in September. Jamie had even been allotted a minor role. When September came, Eugene moved across the road to board with the Rippins, who had three attractive daughters. James paid his board and a dollar a week for his personal allowance, making payments directly to Mrs. Rippin. If sad experience had taught him not to trust his son with money, one ought not to blame him. Yet a dollar a week seems mean.

Eugene did not have much to do except try to write or flirt a little with the Rippin girls. They liked him, but kept their heads. He did not have the money to take out girls. He looked after his health as he had been taught, slept outside on a porch all winter, and went for icy dips in Long Island Sound. But he wrote six one-act plays and a long one during that winter of 1913–14. What is more important is that they were already characteristic. *Fog* may serve as an example.

The action takes place in a lifeboat in which three people are adrift, almost without hope of rescue. The Businessman represents material values, the Poet creative art, and the Peasant Woman with her Dead Child blind faith. Eventually a ship rescues them, guided to them through the fog by the crying of the Dead Child, which seems to represent a mystical triumph and goes unheard by Businessman or Poet. *Fog* is a queer piece, heavy with symbolism, concerned with a conflict of values, but chiefly remarkable for its atmosphere. Fog broods over it like Fate. The true conflict is not between Businessman and Poet, but between both of them and Death. What is the crying of the Child which rescues them? *Fog* may be a poor play, but its concerns are not trivial. In the best of the other plays, *Thirst, Warnings,* and *The Web,* one may see the same antagonism between the individual and his fate, the same intensity. Some rather crude melodrama, always a temptation of O'Neill's, is transformed in these plays by his aspirations. In *Recklessness,* so far his weakest effort, he gives us the melodrama by itself and it is ridiculous. He seldom made that mistake later on.

James O'Neill came back from tour in the spring of 1914 and actually put down good money to have Eugene's plays published. They did not make a sensation and were not the type of play which James was used to. Through his many connections, he could get Eugene's work read. Production was out of the question. He therefore pointed out that Eugene, who had been out of the sanitarium for a year and might be considered perfectly well, ought to get a job.

Eugene was far from willing. He had found his lifework, and money was entirely incidental. He was forced to get out of New London, however, and he thought of an excuse.

Professor George Pierce Baker at Harvard had been

giving a postgraduate course in playwriting for about ten years. He did not claim to turn out dramatists, though he had done so, but to teach the rules and techniques to those who could use them. During the course, each student wrote a one-act play and a long one. He could also submit other pieces for criticism.

James was persuaded to pay, inadequately, as Eugene thought. It is difficult to know how much Eugene got from eight months at Harvard. He was not at his best in a class and generally grunted when asked for a comment. He felt he knew as much about the theater as the professor, which may have been the truth. Neither of the works he wrote for the class was very successful. He showed *Bound East for Cardiff* to Baker, who said it was not really a play. Perhaps what Eugene learned best was a technique of working, a way of getting a rough draft on paper and shaping it into an actual play. No spark was struck, however. Baker recognized no mighty genius in him, but he did select him as one of four to go on another year. Eugene, for his part, intended to return right up to a few days before the opening of school. However, whether from a whim of his father's or his own, he went to New York.

He had taken a job as dramatic critic on a magazine which never got off the ground. Like everyone else of his sort who wanted a cheap lodging, he had made for Greenwich Village, to which his friend Louis Halliday had already introduced him.

It was in the early years of this century that Greenwich Village began to merge as a center of modern ideas. Several things contributed to this. New York, the hub of the business world, attracted writers who were eager for national fame, and in particular those daring spirits who found the provinces dull. Greenwich Village, pleasingly irregular in design, appealed to people who were tired of the monotony of Main Streets or of parallel avenues, all numbered. It was an older part of New York, containing well-built, spacious houses now degenerating into apartments and frankly into slums. The population was to a large extent Italian and colorful. It had the atmosphere, in fact, of a European town and afforded an occasional glimpse of European charm. Rents were very cheap. For thirty dollars a month one could rent a whole floor consisting of tall and handsome rooms with fireplaces. These would have been hastily converted into a dwelling unit. It was rather pleasant than otherwise to find one's bath on a platform beside the kitchen sink, or possibly installed in stately grandeur in what might well have served as a double bedroom. For those who could not afford so much, there were humbler lodgings for eight or ten dollars a month, facilities consisting of a kitchen sink, and a privy in the back yard.

Into such rooms crowded the struggling writers and artists who had come from towns which did not provide friends of their own caliber. But since their living quarters were in most cases unsuitable for entertaining, they depended on public places of meeting. These, in turn, being open to all, drew everyone together and discouraged the formation of cliques. Presently the Village acquired its own point of view. Everybody knew everyone else. All shared the new ideas of the time and a love of informal living. All that was necessary to meet fellow-artists and writers was the will to do so. Most were young and not particularly famous. The general public was so far content to let them alone.

The chief meeting places of this intelligentsia were Mabel Dodge's and Polly Halliday's. These were very different. Mabel—Mrs. Dodge—was a wealthy woman bored with the conventional distractions of entertainment and travel. Establishing herself near Washington Square, she got to know Hutchins Hapgood, a fairly successful journalist, who introduced her to everybody. The Dodge mansion was soon flung open to the Village. Evening entertainments began to take the form of set discussions in which conventions—moral, political, artistic—were derided. Freud, Marx, Cubism, the Russian ballet, expressionist drama, and other importations from Europe stimulated thought. Anybody who had ideas to express was always welcome.

Polly Halliday, more informal, ran a restaurant. She came from Evanston, Illinois, and was an anarchist. In those days before the Russian revolution, anarchism held the extreme left-wing position in the political world which Communism holds today. Anarchist theory was born in opposition to the rigid conservative governments of Russia and eastern Europe. It consisted in opposing restrictions of all sorts on individual liberty. In theory, anarchists were against all governments. Their extremist members had an international reputation for sabotage and bombing outrages. The doctrine had been brought to America by political exiles, one of whom Polly Halliday had married. Hippolyte Havel was a little, mustached, bespectacled Austrian with a goatee beard who had a long record of imprisonment for political offenses in Europe. Under a more liberal regime in America, he had married Polly, and now obliged as a waiter in the semi-basement where Polly cooked. But though his actions were tamer, his opinions were still colorful. "Bourgeois pigs!" he would snarl audibly as he slapped plates down containing the solid, cheap dinner which was Polly's great attraction.

Hippolyte was all bark and no bite these days, while Polly was warmhearted. Presently her enterprise expanded into part of the Liberal Club. A couple of upstairs floors of the usual rundown, dignified sort were taken and furnished with wooden tables and chairs. Cubist and futurist art, mostly unsalable, found a home on the walls. There was an upright electric piano, and on Fridays for a quarter one could get a glass of wine while tunes were banged out for dancing. There was even a strip of grass behind for summer evenings, and city ordinances about noise were not strict. Actually Friday was no noisier than other nights, and arguments were often just as loud as the piano. Next door was the Washington Square Bookshop, kept by the Boni brothers, publishers of Joyce's *Ulysses*. Presently a door was hacked through between the two, presumably in the hopes that Liberal Club members would buy in Boni's shop. What actually happened, however, was that the door presented the Liberal Club with a free library. Instead of standing uncomfortably in Boni's peering into the latest publications, members could take them into the club, whence they did not always find their way back to the shelves. In fact, the club premises were a magnet to Greenwich Villagers. There was always something going on in them.

Polly naturally was not without rivals. She had her imitators, while for more serious drinking there were saloons. Of these, two were especially popular. The Golden Swan, known to the Village as the Hell-Hole, was a tough and dirty joint whose proprietor experimented with a pig in the cellar as a garbage dispose-all. He offered a free lunch with a five-cent beer and was popular with those who were out of luck. When they were in funds again, they naturally went back. In the long run, the Golden Swan was never out of pocket. Its back room was also the headquarters of a New York gang called the Hudson Dusters, but as a general rule the two groups did not mix. O'Connor's, whose ladies' bar was dubbed "The Working Girl's Home," was a similar place. O'Connor had employed Masefield the poet as a barman when the latter was on his travels. He liked to talk about Masefield and was also famous for his skill at ejecting a noisy customer by squirting soda water in his face.

This was a different part of town from Eugene's old hangout near the docks, or even from the hotel where the family stayed while James was in town. It was not unknown to Eugene, however. Louis Halliday had introduced him to some of its colorful characters. In the last year or two he had met Jack Reed, who used to be called "The Golden Boy of the Village." Immensely able, Reed was already a famous foreign correspondent. In fact, he was different in every superficial way from the shy Eugene, to whom he was attracted by their common rebelliousness of temperament.

Thus sponsored, it would have been possible for Eugene to enter into the life of the Village. Its ways, however, were too social for him. Besides, he was still oppressed by his personal problems. His plays did not interest producers and were never likely to, yet Eugene did not consider them spare-time activity. They were his lifework, and he angrily resisted pressure from James to get a job. Faced with the necessity of compromising on this vital point, he turned as usual back to whisky.

This time the scene of his orgies was the Hell-Hole. He had progressed to the point where he no longer considered himself a down-and-out seaman. Or perhaps he simply feared tuberculosis. At all events, he did not go back to Jimmy-the-Priest's. The Hell-Hole was perhaps a little better in that the company was not all hopeless. Yet it was not the Liberal Club after all. There were more down-and-out drunkards in the Hell-Hole than intellectuals, and there were the Hudson Dusters as well. The Dusters were an Irish gang who terrorized the neighborhood, black-mailing the local merchants for supplies. As a general rule, they moved in a different orbit from the Village intellectuals, but they took to Eugene. He was Irish, for one thing; and he felt at home with them. He impressed them by a nonchalant ease in their company. He was different, and yet he never made them feel that he was slumming.

This was the more remarkable because, though never condemning, he took no part in their activities. One of them, seeing him wear newspapers inside his jacket to keep warm, told him to go uptown and pick out the overcoat he wanted in any of the big stores, and that he would lift it. Eugene simply smiled and shook his head. In Buenos Aires when he was destitute, an acquaintance had suggested they stage a holdup together. Again he had refused. His war with society was not of this type. It was an extension of his unbearable personal problems, and he could only fight it within himself. Even the legitimate activities of left-wing Villagers were not his affair. He combined a fierce dislike of the society into which he had been born with a determination to do nothing about it.

Those who knew him at this time shook their heads over Eugene. They thought he was drinking himself to death. Presently he drifted in his aimless way into the company of Terry Carlin.

Terry Carlin was a tall, gaunt, impressive-looking man who had long ago resigned from work as a protest against the inhumanity of the capitalist system. This he had experienced first-hand, being the son of poor Irish parents and forced into work under sweatshop conditions at ten years old. Self-educated and with remarkable, if strange, abilities, Terry lived in the Village on his charm. He was a fascinating talker and existed on free drinks from his friends, free lunches at the Hell-Hole, and an occasional bed there when various methods of finding a place to sleep were unavailing. Terry posed as a disbeliever in human nature, quite unshockable, but powerless to interfere or help. He had been an anarchist, but had given that up. What was left to him was a deep compassion for the slum-dwelling poor and a capacity to express his disillusion in words.

Terry was at once good and bad for Eugene. They had in common their Irish backgrounds and lost Catholic faith. They both admired the philosophy of Nietzsche. They both had great sensitivity, and of a similar sort. They were bleeding inwardly for mankind. Their problems might be, and in Eugene's case certainly were, personal. Out of these, however, both had gained deeper understanding, especially of the poor. Both were struggling to comprehend the meaning of life itself. They had both degraded themselves to the simplest physical level and learned to feel at home with down-and-outers. There, however, the resemblance ceased. Terry Carlin had achieved a certain content with his life. He drank. He was filthy. He slept where he could and did not mind. In fact, he prided himself on having risen above material comforts. Eugene, much younger, far more intense, was hiding from life. He was plunging deliberately deep, too deep, it might be feared, for recovery. Terry Carlin lived to eighty years of age. O'Neill on his present course would have been dead by thirty.

O'Neill learned a great deal from Terry, who had the ability to put into words what the younger man was feeling. He had also practiced surviving on nothing a year, which was what Eugene was trying to do. Terry would get a presentable friend to look at apartments and press a lump of clay against the door latch of a suitable empty one to prevent it from locking. Then Terry and O'Neill would move in with mattresses and books and bottles of whisky. Failing mattresses, they spread newspapers on the floor. They lived on the Hell-Hole's lunch and on sacks of oysters which they bought at Fulton Fish Market because they were cheap and needed no cooking. Eugene was not entirely without money. James left him a dollar every day with the cashier of his own hotel on Twenty-seventh Street. But Eugene did not go in to see his father when he picked up this allowance. The money went on liquor.

Aimless though his life appeared, he had not lost all sense of purpose. Jig Cook and his Provincetown group had started acting a few small plays of their own the preceding summer. They were now back in the Village and talking excitedly about founding a native American theater. They wanted plays of an experimental sort and were proposing a regular summer season in Provincetown. O'Neill made no approach to them, though it must have been hard for him to avoid their notice, since Village circles were small. Yet, dubious but inquiring, he prepared to drift up to Cape Cod with Terry Carlin, who had camped out there during previous summers. In later life, O'Neill did not suggest that he had anything special in mind when he decided to visit Provincetown in that summer of 1916. It stands to reason, however, that his presence was no fantastic coincidence. Better be performed for a fifty-cent entrance fee on a remote strip of sand off the coast of Massachusetts than never be performed at all.

Terry and he established themselves in the shelter of an abandoned boat on the Truro shore, and they very soon ran out of money. Hutchins Hapgood, one of the Province-town group, was a particular friend of Terry's and also a newspaper man with a paying job. Terry undertook to walk over and ask him for ten dollars. Eugene came too, quite possibly to oversee its expenditure, since Terry was capable of getting drunk and returning a few days later with pockets empty. Once the money was safely in hand, Eugene went home, while Terry lingered to greet his Village friends.

Presently he ran into Susan Glaspell, obsessed by the problem which her husband had made for the time his sole concern. "Terry, don't you have a play to read to us?" There was after all a hobo poet of considerable prominence in the Village. Why not a hobo playwright?

"You know I don't, Susan," Terry protested. "I never write. I just think, and sometimes I talk. . . . But young Mr. O'Neill, who has come up here with me, has a trunkful of plays."

Susan had never heard of young Mr. O'Neill, and she was not favorably impressed by a trunkful of probable rejects. But, leaving no stone unturned, she asked Terry to tell Mr. O'Neill to bring some of his plays to her house that evening. He came, and with him he brought *Bound East for Cardiff*. It was a moment of opportunity, and George Cook seized it.

5   THE BIRTH OF THE LITTLE THEATERS

It was now 1916, and O'Neill had been writing ever since he got out of Gaylord Sanitarium three years before. James O'Neill had really tried to take an interest in the first constructive efforts of his son. He had read some of Eugene's plays and had not liked them. The gloomy tone and heavy symbolism of *Fog* was not calculated to appeal to a man who had made a fortune from *Monte Cristo*. It lacked, he was bound to think, box-office appeal. All the same, James had made efforts to use his connections to get Eugene's plays noticed. George Tynan, who was a Broadway producer of that time, recalled later that James had given him plays of his son's and that he had returned them, either unread or after a quick glance, with some smooth words about showing promise, but needing time and practice to develop.

Eugene himself had been no more successful in selling his work. When he sent manuscripts in, he had them returned to him a year later after the producer went bankrupt, still in the original wrappers and unopened. An intermediary had presented some of his work to the actor-manager of the Princess Theater, which performed modern plays, though chiefly from Europe. His response was no more enthusiastic than Tynan's. Eugene had received some encouragement, but never from anyone whose praise could directly lead to a production.

He had been anxious to get his plays published, hoping, no doubt, that he might appeal to a wider public. But when James O'Neill had paid for the production of a volume in 1914, it had fallen disappointingly flat. There was a favorable review from a friend of James's who did genuinely admire his son's work. Sales, however, were practically nonexistent. The O'Neills gave away a good many copies, and the remainder were offered to the author at thirty cents each. Without hesitation he turned them down, thereby missing an opportunity of making a handsome sum later on.

Discouragement could not turn Eugene from his purpose, but it had helped to drive him back to drink. It did, however, disillusion James O'Neill, who still clung to the

73

notion that his sons ought to support themselves. He thought it unlikely that Eugene's unpleasant plays would ever succeed. The boy ought to get a job. The extreme poverty which Eugene was sharing with Terry Carlin in 1916 was the result of father's and son's refusal to compromise.

The trouble was that young O'Neill, who a few years later appeared the mirror of his times, was at the moment in advance of the theatrical world. American drama had not up to this time made any pretense of being art. European drama had been for a generation in the heyday of a tremendous revival which, starting with Ibsen and Strindberg, had spread through all the principal languages of Europe. In English alone, Shaw, Galsworthy, Yeats, Synge, and a crowd of oncoming writers in London and Dublin were making the era a notable one. In America, no original dramatic talent had been so far discovered.

The reason for this did not lie in any lack of popular enthusiasm. The whole career of James O'Neill is a proof of the endless appetite for drama which Americans showed all over the country. People in the fast-growing American towns were really hard put to it to find an acceptable form of public entertainment in the days before movies and radio. Distances from other centers were great. Immigrants missed the pageantry of church and state to which they were accustomed in Europe. There were consequently theaters in every fair-sized town and acting companies without end. Railroads were going in, and better communications steadily increased the size of audiences.

In the days when James O'Neill got his first chance to

walk on-stage in *Colleen Bawn*, all the better local theaters possessed their own companies and, of course, played repertory. But stars came on tour, too, bringing with them neither their company nor its costumes. The star simply played his own successful role, Hamlet, some villainous villain, or noble savage. The local company fitted in around him as best it could. In this fashion, James O'Neill as a young man had opportunity to form his style on the model of the best actors of his time. He was also accustomed to a variety of roles in a repertoire of plays which he was constantly enlarging.

By the time that James married Ella, this situation had more or less broken down. Better communications made it possible for whole companies to go on tour, while larger audiences made a theatrical hit immensely profitable. Small places which could hardly support their own repertory gave ready welcome to a traveling troupe in an auditorium which could be used for lectures and vaudeville shows as well. *Monte Cristo* provides a good example of what happened. Audiences were growing more sophisticated and did demand better scenery, production, and acting standards. All these could be met by a traveling company performing the same play for as long as it paid.

In the course of James's lifetime, theater business became big business. Expenses began to soar as well as profits. Theater buildings had to improve as productions became more complex. This raised rents. Transport of costumes and properties became elaborate. Actors, now engaged only for the life of a play, must look forward to periods of unemployment between productions. In compensation, they naturally demanded higher pay. Such tendencies were exaggerated in New York by its fantastic growth, the increasing amount people were willing to pay for seats, the activities of ticket speculators, and the steep rise in real-estate values. It became possible not merely to win a great fortune with a play, but to lose one. Meanwhile, big booking syndicates made tight connections between a run on Broadway and a successful tour.

In circumstances such as these, producers on Broadway were unwilling to take the smallest risk. Each play they adopted was as like the last smashing hit as they could make it. Their eye was on the mass audience with which they were familiar. Their formula was light comedy or sentimental drama, as far as possible removed from the realities of life. Taste was changing, it is true. In cautious fashion, producers recognized the fact. America was saturated at long last with *Monte Cristo*. But from the producers' point of view, a change of taste did not mean a change of purpose. Audiences still came to the theater to relax and be lifted out of themselves. Success depended on keeping abreast of the most recent way to do this.

How cut and dried the conventions had become may be seen by an experience of O'Neill's while he was attending Professor Baker's drama class at Harvard in 1914 and 1915. Augustus Thomas, then a highly successful playwright, took over the class for two morning sessions while he explained how to write a Broadway hit.

You first choose a star for whose talents you will write your play. Since the class chose an older woman, an emotional actress, it was decided she would be a mother threatened with losing her child. With the help of the class, detail was quickly added. Let her live in a Puritan New England community, where the townsfolk discover she had had a lover and decided she is not a fit mother for her child. There must be a great emotional scene where she defends her right to keep it . . . and so on and so forth. Thomas concluded by promising that if the class wrote up this plot as a scenario, he would put dialogue to it and guarantee a production. O'Neill, and for once one can hardly blame him, went straight off to Boston and got drunk.

Fed this kind of corn, the American theater presented a pattern which is familiar to us from Hollywood. Actor and playwright were in the hands of speculators out to make a glittering fortune by obvious means. The modern American novel had already started on its interesting career. People were not writing serious drama because the chances of getting it produced were nonexistent. O'Neill in his obstinacy chose to disregard the facts and say what he pleased. But O'Neill was the exception, not the rule.

The Little Theater movement was the first outcome of a rising discontent with these conditions. Why should not the exciting works of the great Europeans be shown more often on this side of the Atlantic? If there was no vast audience, there certainly was a small one. If the professional would not do the job, what about the amateur? The continuing flood of immigrants contained a minority of educated folk who knew good drama. There was talk about the repertory theaters of Europe. These flourished, partly by patronage and long tradition, partly because centers were closer together and repertory theaters had a wider

cultural audience to draw on. They were content, moreover, to be small. A modest income and an international
reputation satisfied them. They did not aspire to the great
fortunes made on Broadway.

In 1912, the Chicago Little Theater and the Toy
Theater in Boston were both opened. These might best be
described as semi-professional. Small salaries were paid out
of low admissions, and serious plays were produced. They
both got off to a flying start, inspired by the national tour
of the Abbey Theatre from Dublin.

Even among the art theaters of Europe, the Abbey
Theatre held a special place. It was at once mother and
child of an Irish literature which had hardly existed a generation earlier. Irish drama was not a revival. It was, sub-
stantially, a new product and had basic national materials
to draw on. Romantic, poetic, only slightly touched by in-
dustrialization, it had fresh themes in Irish legend and in
the life of Irish peasantry. It was not, however, behind the
times. Cultured Irishmen might as yet be a small group,
but they had behind them all the resources of the English
language. They had shared in the ferment which was
changing the nature of drama and poetry. Standing with
their feet on Irish soil, they looked at once forward and
backward. The Abbey Theatre had been founded to focus
the efforts of this artistic group. Without it, Yeats and
Synge, for instance, might have remained purely poets;
and we should have had to do without *Riders to the Sea*
and *The Playboy of the Western World*. Lesser, but still
considerable talents had been attracted also, though
O'Casey's *Juno and the Paycock* was still to come. Indeed,

the whole point of the Abbey Theatre was that it inspired the national drama it presented.

The case of the Abbey Theatre was well put forward in America. The troupe brought with it a sample of its leading supporters, people of distinguished names in the Irish world of letters. These gave excellent talks on the ideas behind the theater and how it had consolidated a revived national life. People interested in drama flocked to listen, among them, as we have noted before, Eugene O'Neill. It was the period when young Eugene seemed an utter derelict. He had occasionally thought of writing drama, but had formed no definite purpose yet. He was living as far as he could on nothing at all except liquor. Yet he found energy to go uptown and watch or listen.

The visit of O'Neill to the Abbey Theatre seems more significant if we look back now than it was at the time. It inspired him with no resolve; and if at Gaylord two years later he thought of it again, we know nothing of this. But whether or not his visit had any direct effect on his life, its indirect one was to be great. Among those who attended its performances was George Cram Cook, not yet acquainted with O'Neill or even the Village. The 1916 meeting between the two men in Provincetown came about and later became fruitful because of the inspiration Cook had derived in part from the Abbey Theatre.

George Cram Cook, who was destined to introduce O'Neill to the American public, was a large, gregarious man in his middle forties with an impressive presence, a massive head, and abundant hair with one long lock prematurely gray. Son of a well-to-do and conventional Iowa lawyer, he had been brought up by his mother to fulfill artistic inspirations which had been stifled in her by a prosaic marriage. Young George, as it turned out, had considerable talents in such a variety of fields that it was not easy to decide how his genius should express itself. By 1912, he had tried a great many things and failed in them all. He had published a poor historical novel and a ponderous one about philosophical ideas. He had thrown up college teaching because he would not cram facts into a course or even confine himself to the subject he was supposed to cover. He had tried a combination of farming and philosophy, which led to more failure. He had struggled with alcoholism once and even, briefly, with madness. He had been married twice and was now waiting for his second divorce in order to marry Susan Glaspell.

So far, George Cook had not made anything out of his life. Notwithstanding, he was a man who fascinated many. To talk with him was in itself an education. He had the capacity to rouse enthusiasm and stimulate ideas. Great plans came into his head. He would sit in the center of a group, running his hands through his hair and twisting his gray forelock as he developed some splendid conception. The stars would pale in the sky, and nobody would think of going to bed. Yet hitherto none of these thoughts had been translated into action.

Perhaps the best way of explaining Jig Cook's fascination is to tell a story about him. Traveling in Italy, he struck up a friendship with two Italian soldiers on a train going to Rome. The three of them spent three weeks in Rome together touring the town. Eventually the time came for Jig to leave. They were sitting over a bottle of wine on their last evening and began to talk of Time as the great enemy of human relationships. They three were friends and had learned to know one another intimately. Their time together had now gone by, and after this evening they would probably never meet again. They made a bargain to defy Time. It should not exist for their friendship. If ever they did chance to meet, they would greet one another as though they had parted the preceding evening. Even more, they would go on with their present argument on the merits of Dante and Shakespeare, just as though Time had not interrupted.

Twenty years went by, and Jig for some reason or other went to a meeting at Northwestern University. There in the hall was a man he thought he recognized. It seemed incredible, but he went straight up to him and made a remark on Dante versus Shakespeare.

The other stared at him. "I beg your pardon!"

Jig repeated himself.

The man said stiffly, "You must have taken me for someone else."

"I beg *your* pardon," Jig said in his turn. "Are you not Signor So-and-So? Don't you remember how we met in Rome and took a vow that we would defy Time?"

Now the man remembered and was delighted. But the result was disappointing. He ought to have deserted Northwestern and his business in order to find a café table and a cheap bottle of red wine. They ought to have sat arguing till sunrise. "Instead," said Jig in disgust, "he tried to introduce me to his wife and daughter!"

Typical of Jig in this incident were not merely the good conversation, memorable after so long a time, but the fantastic quality of the bargain that was struck and his observance of it. He really expected the man to leave his wife and daughter and disappear with him. He himself would have done it. He entered into ideas with his whole self.

Such was the man who was fired by the lectures on the Abbey Theatre. They crystallized in his mind an idea of the theater which had been vaguely present ever since he had studied Greek drama at Harvard many years before. It was not coincidence, he had felt, that the city of Athens had produced four mighty dramatists in the space of a couple of generations, not to mention numerous others whose works have not survived, though they were then considered of comparable merit. Athenian drama had flourished because the conditions were right. It had grown, as it were, out of the soil. Its conventions, which would be irksome to us today, had been fruitful because they belonged to religious rituals embedded in the national tradition. Its great talents had been developed because the whole life of the city was focused on drama. Athenian lads aspired to dance in the choruses; wealthy Athenians produced the plays out of love of their city. The people gave up some days every year to judging them. In fact, its drama was an expression of the spirit of Athens. It is on occasions when the pulse of national life and national drama beat as one, Jig felt, that great plays are produced. The very fact that drama calls for a combination of actor, artist, dancer, musician, playwright, and producer fits it in a peculiar way to express the spirit of its times. The Abbey Theatre was doing in its modern fashion what the Greeks had done.

In this way, the idea took root in Jig's mind that the American theater ought to arise out of American life. He conceived of it in a sense as learning by doing. No need to sit back and wait for plays worth producing. No need either to put on the great European plays, no matter how novel or important these might be. Get American talents concerned in producing plays, and plays would be written.

These ideas filled Jig Cook's mind in 1912, but he took no step to put them into action. They remained just another of his theories while he disentangled his personal life. His divorce went through. He married Susan Glaspell and moved to Greenwich Village. Susan Glaspell, who was an Iowa girl and had for a long time been part of Jig's circle, had succeeded as a magazine writer and a novelist of a more popular sort than Jig Cook. She was already established in the Village and had joined the society of those who summered in Provincetown. Thus without the necessity of breaking much ice, the Cooks plunged immediately into the stimulating life of the Village. While Eugene was at Gaylord Sanitarium, New London, and Harvard, Jig Cook was finding his feet.

There was plenty going on in Greenwich Village. Indeed, for a man of George Cook's temperament there was almost too much to absorb. *The Masses*, for instance, a lively left-wing newspaper, had as assistant editor Floyd Dell, an old friend of Jig's in Iowa and Chicago. These were the days of the first large-scale strikes in America and of their repression by strong-arm methods which would outrage us today. Mary Vorse and Joe O'Brien, both writers of socialist views, had actually fallen in love and married after a meeting while both were reporting a strike in Massachusetts. The winter of 1913–14 was a time of depression; and destitute men began raiding the churches as places to sleep in. Arrests followed. The O'Briens took up the cause of the homeless. Money was raised and a committee was formed. Thereafter, church raiding took on an organized quality. It served as a protest against society's callousness. O'Brien, too, was on the editorial board of *The Masses*, and the paper crusaded for the unemployed in days when no help was given them by the state.

A strike of silkworkers in Paterson, New Jersey, led to a vast pageant staged by John Reed in Madison Square Garden. Reed, one of the ablest newspapermen of his generation, imported a thousand strikers from Paterson to present in skillful, pageant form their whole story, acted out by the workers themselves. This startling tour de force, almost in itself a folk drama, was followed up in *The Masses* by articles and cartoons full of dramatic fire.

Jig Cook, as a member of the Liberal Club and intimate of Floyd Dell, was in touch with these events. He had in an earlier day flirted with socialism. He was, however, by temperament far more fitted for aesthetic or moral reforms than political ones. Jig was fumbling with something large and vague, the position of man in his universe, the highest strivings of his nature. Nor had he forgotten his ideas on drama. The theatrical world off Broadway was not entirely barren. The Henry Street Settlement had been for some years putting on plays and was shortly to establish the Neighborhood Theater. Various national groups—Jewish, German, even Chinese—presented their own plays. There was a Negro group, giving outlet to the talent of its people. Jig and Susan attended various productions, attributing their vitality to their connections with their players' national roots.

Jig theorized largely, but he made no effort to put anything into practice. He was new to the Village and feeling his way. He was dizzy with unaccustomed stimulus and still uncertain what to take up. Thus when the Liberal Club decided to branch out into a dramatic group, the moving spirit was not Jig Cook, but his friend Floyd Dell, who had also seen the Abbey Players in Chicago.

As assistant editor of *The Masses*, Dell had immense authority in the Village. It is not surprising that the club chose his play to put on, a marital comedy concerning a Spanish hidalgo and a gypsy. It is fair to say that it had certain merits. Dell's writing was always clever. However, it had been chosen in competition with other playlets whose authors, individualistic Villagers, felt disgruntled. There were also more would-be actors than parts. Ida Rauh, a handsome, dramatic, highly cultured young woman who was married to Max Eastman, chief editor of *The Masses*, was one of the malcontents. On the day of the performance, she happened to sit next to Lawrence Langner, a youngish patent attorney who was discovering a new, intense life in the Village. She told him she could have played a gypsy better, and he replied that he would have made a better hidalgo. Encouraged by each other's sympathy, they talked freely afterward, finding others to agree with their criticisms. One of the Boni brothers from the bookshop, who was acquainted with the Chicago Little Theater, told them they ought to go ahead and strike out for themselves.

The notion took root. Lawrence Langner was making money, not much in terms of big theatrical ventures, but a great deal compared to most Village incomes. A few other people proved willing to back the venture. A small theater building in the neighborhood proved rentable. In this way the Washington Square Theater came into being for the purpose of producing one-act plays of a more interesting nature than the current musicals on Broadway.

This looked something like Jig Cook's ideal theater, and he supported it with enthusiasm. In fact, he played a curious role in its opening stages. Before the curtain went up on the early performances, Jig, a large and conspicuous man, complained in angry tones. Susan looked embarrassed and said "Shsh!" The more she hushed, the noisier Jig got. It was already quarter to nine, he said, and he did not propose to wait much longer for a bunch of amateurs. By this time, the whole audience was looking at him. The incident was supposed to lead up to a before-the-curtain speech by the producer, pretending to pacify Jig by a little explanation of what the theater was trying to do. This comedy was played out every night to the distress of Susan, who got so tired of her own role that she used to call up friends and ask them if they would like to be Jig's "wife" for the night.

The Washington Square Theater did not do badly. Considering that its audience was small and its admission only fifty cents, it was hardly expected to make much money. Presently it was able to allow tiny salaries to its chief actors, a bare living wage in Village terms. After putting on many short plays, it was swallowed up by World War I. Langner's time was completely taken up by his patent business, and similar problems beset the other backers. It reopened after the war, but in a different fashion which was also destined to make theatrical history and to play a big part in the life of Eugene O'Neill.

THE WASHINGTON SQUARE THEATER was an important step in the new direction. It did not, however, satisfy Jig Cook once the first enthusiasm had worn off. Nor was it advanced enough to be the introducer of O'Neill to his theatrical public. The truth was, the Washington Square Theater was in a certain sense a rival to Broadway. It had a professional point of view and expected to keep going by attracting an audience. Langner and its other backers were not made of money. Thus, though it appealed to the off-

Broadway theatrical groups, it did retain a certain timidity. No one could call Eugene O'Neill skillful at advertising himself. He was, however, passionately anxious to have a play produced; and yet he never approached the Washington Square Theater at this stage. He surely would have done so had he not been convinced that his efforts would be useless.

The Washington Square Theater was very conscious that it had to feel its way if it was to remain solvent. In order to do so, it had to consider its potential market. Weighing plays in terms of audience appeal, its sponsors felt, was only reasonable. Village extremists did not agree. O'Neill, whose habit was to avoid what he did not like, was not sympathetic to the efforts of the little theater either. It was obvious that he could not now and might not ever make money himself. Almost two years were to pass before he was to have his opportunity, once and for all.

The Washington Square Theater soon had a group of critics more vociferous than O'Neill. Ida Rauh broke with Lawrence Langner. After the fiasco of his play when the corpse sat up, she was not offered another good role. She attributed this to spite. Langner maintained that her acting was affected and that she was too old to play the ingenue. However this may be, her influence, which had already proved itself strong, was on the side of the malcontents.

Jig Cook was by now ready to join them. Along with his high ideals, Cook had a large amount of personal vanity. Both were soon offended. In the first blush of his enthusiasm, he had applied for Susan's help in putting together a one-act play. Neither of them had done such a thing before, but they felt that the result was really not bad. It would not be fair to say that Susan Glaspell took to playwriting as a duck takes to water. Actually, she wrote few plays that she was not pressured into and seemed to turn back with relief to her long novels. Yet it was clear from the start that the form suited her. She had to compress and clarify. She could not overwrite in the sentimental way which tempted her. Some of her short stories were proving good for similar reasons. On the whole, Jig and Susan were pleased with their play.

It was a take-off on the psychological jargon which was the latest thing. Freud had taken the Village by storm. Everybody must have his complex. Everything was charged with inner meaning. In the turmoil of self-examination normal to the creative spirits of the Village, psychology fitted naturally into place. Meanwhile, the newness of its ideas gave importance to the most farfetched applications of theory. Jig and Susan's masterpiece presents Henrietta tiresomely pestering her husband Stephen to do something about his complexes. Presently she is visited by her sister Mabel, who has made an unromantic but not specially unhappy marriage. Poor Mabel, her head full of imaginary troubles, is persuaded to visit a psychiatrist. He reveals to her that her urges demand Stephen. Henrietta's doctrine always has been that urges must be satisfied at all costs. She loves Stephen, however, and is not willing to give him up. He sees his advantage and strikes a bargain. Henrietta promises to leave his complexes alone, and he joins her in persuading poor simple Mabel to go back home to her husband.

It is easy to see that this is no great play, but it reads well. To be sure, psychology has come of age since that day, and much of the humor in consequence seems naïve. But certainly for its time, within the framework of the one-act play, and in comparison with others being written in the Village, *Suppressed Desires* was not bad. At all events, it was far more likely to succeed than *Fog* and similar efforts of O'Neill's. Jig regarded his masterpiece with a prejudiced eye, but he had reason to think it was worth a production. Great was his indignation when the little theaters turned it down. "Too special!" they said. "No audience yet for that idea!"

Jig was furious. It was painful to fumble endlessly for a means of self-expression, only to have a good little play brushed off by the very institutions which had been founded to encourage fresh ideas. But unlike O'Neill, he was prepared to do something about it. Meanwhile, however, he talked. The bane of drama was this notion of audience appeal. Good plays would make their own audience. He was sure of it. The job of the little theaters was not to please people, but to stimulate playwriting. They ought to be putting on experiments, the wilder the better. They ought if necessary to let authors fumble. Sooner or later the meeting of ideas which is bound to take place in a theatrical production would of itself produce excellence. In fact, they should be bringing out new talent, not turning it away. Jig's theoretical views and the personal slight from which he was suffering both led him to the same conclusion. The Washington Square Theater was not that ideal focus of talent which the Abbey Theatre had proved. It was not worthy of the Greek ideal in modern form. Nothing would come of it.

By this time, Jig was already a personage in the Village. To be sure, his influence was strongest among those who also summered in Provincetown. On the whole these tended to include the aesthetic rather than the political sort of Villager, simply because these latter found themselves less at ease outside New York. It happened, therefore, in the summer of 1915, that Provincetown contained, besides Jig Cook and Susan Glaspell, another rejected playwright. Neith Boyce, the attractive wife of Hutchins Hapgood, was a novelist of approximately Susan Glaspell's caliber. In other words, she was of second rank, but enjoyed her following and was thought to have promise.

In the outburst of enthusiasm for drama which had swept over Greenwich Village, Neith Boyce had also written a play. *Constancy*, though inferior to *Suppressed Desires*, was another good example of a one-act play written for an intelligent audience. It, too, had been turned down. Neith Boyce and, what was perhaps more important, her husband desired to see it produced. Ida Rauh, who wanted to act, was also in Provincetown. It was not long before these people persuaded themselves and their intimates that they ought to produce the two plays.

Jig, who was not busy with serious writing, was on fire with enthusiasm. The plays were small and the group was amateur, but the idea was basic. Authors should produce their own plays out of sheer enjoyment. There were modernistic painters among their friends who could contribute to the sets. There was even someone anxious to revolutionize stage design. Robert Edmond Jones had studied what was being done abroad. He had real ability and had just begun to make himself a name. Considering the talent that was available in Greenwich Village, it is perhaps not surprising that in one area at least the Players commanded someone of the very first class.

In this way the Provincetown Players came together, partly as a group of friends all interested in drama, and partly, as they were to call themselves later, a Playwright's Theater. It was natural that the two authors should direct his or her play. The acting company, with the exception of Ida Rauh and the Ballantines, was amateur. The sets had the free services of a couple of modern artists as well as Robert Edmond Jones. The expenses were only those sketchy ones involving purchase of minor articles which could not be borrowed. Lights and furniture were of the simplest sort. The audience consisted merely of such people as could be gathered by invitation. The performance took place in the Hapgood home. The auditorium was the living room, furnished with borrowed chairs. The first play was performed on the porch. For the second, the audience was asked to turn its chairs and face the arch looking into the dining room.

All went well, in fact exceedingly well. For the actors, the plays had been the highpoint of the summer so far. The authors, who had directed their own productions, had a sense of having expressed themselves. The audience boasted of the occasion to such an extent that various people who had not been asked wanted to know why. In fact, the spirit of the thing was such that everyone wanted to go on acting.

A great deal of this must have been due to Jig. He had the ability to excite other people about his enthusiasms and had exercised it to the full. He was, in addition, as all who knew him agree, a born teacher. In the production of his little play, his talents fell into place. He took the lead, not merely because it was his play, but because he was a natural leader of men. The individualists of Greenwich Village, whom nobody had been able to organize completely, found themselves possessed of an exciting group spirit. They had not attained any sense of mission yet, but they were willing to devote an extraordinary amount of energy to something which was not within their field of primary endeavor. They had begun to feel that each could contribute to a whole of greater value.

Most of this was not conscious as yet. They were carried along on a wave of enthusiasm which they did not analyze. They determined that they ought to give a bigger performance. Almost opposite the Cooks' house was a dilapidated wharf which had been bought on an impulse by Mary Vorse and was rented to various summer people. At the street end was a largish building which had been a ship chandler's store and contained the family dwelling behind and above. Behind this was the actual wharf with two buildings on it, the first a small fish-packing house which was not too decrepit to house a penniless artist. At the seaward end lay the wharfhouse itself, a tall shed

94

twenty-five feet square, at present rented by Margaret Steele, Wilbur Daniel's wife, as a summer studio. She now offered the place for a more ambitious dramatic performance.

The Lewis wharf was about seventy-five years old and lay exposed at low tide, built out on piles across the sand. When the tide came in, the water lapped underneath with sucking noises, and the salt smells of the sea grew temporarily stronger. The shed was cluttered with Margaret Steele's own gear, a disused boat, and various nets and anchors belonging to people in the town which had been left there, presumably, when their owners went out of business. The wharf had in its heyday accommodated four large schooners and their cargoes from the Grand Banks. It had also functioned as the lumber, coal, and ice wharf for the East End of Provincetown. That old shed had seen many a cargo hauled in through the great door at its seaward end. But the last ship to go to the Grand Banks from Provincetown had made her final voyage in 1913. Long before that the Lewis wharf had only been used by a couple of families to get in fresh fish for the local market. Eventually that business had died away; and Mary Vorse had bought the place for a song.

All in all, it was not a bad spot for the sort of performance Jig and his friends had in mind. To be sure, there was no stage and obviously no lighting. Oil lamps would do, and they had had no raised stage at the Hapgoods'. Since there were no seats, boards were hastily put up on kegs. By now enthusiasm ran high. Jig had actually

95

written another comedy called *Change Your Style*. The arrival of modernistic artists from the village had caused some controversy in Provincetown, which had for a long time been the site of a summer art school run by Charles Hawthorne, a well-known nineteenth-century painter. When postimpressionists and Cubists arrived, one of the artists, Demuth, was observed portraying a yellow sand dune with pink and blue "worms." He caused a sensation. Presently the story went around that when he applied for a dog license, he had been asked his dog's color and had replied, squinting his eyes against the sun to get it right, "Orange with purple spots." Jig's comedy on the rivalry between the two schools had no great merit, but it was topical and would rouse laughter. Wilbur Daniel Steele had also been persuaded to try his hand at a dramatic piece. The action of *Contemporaries* began in the dark. People were apparently talking about the raids which had recently taken place in New York, where the homeless had taken refuge in the churches. The son of a poor family had been led astray by a preacher who had been leading the poor into a church. When the lights went on, the audience discovered that the policeman was a Roman centurion, while the boy's family were Palestine Jews and the preacher, of course, was Jesus.

It poured with rain on the night of their production. People came sloshing down the street with galoshes and umbrellas. Automobiles were not yet common in a place like Provincetown. People got around its three-mile length on foot, or else they waited for the horse-drawn "accommodation," or begged a lift in a cart carrying goods across town. From Truro one might come by boat. However, people came, and wet as they were, the audience gathered. Mary Vorse saw one parked umbrella work itself through a hole in the floor and disappear onto the sand below. Other umbrellas, set in motion by its fall, gradually followed. The danger of a fire had worried the producers, seeing that footlights were lanterns with tin reflectors. Four people were standing by with shovels and sand in case of trouble. During a later performance the wharfhouse did catch fire and two walls were smoke-blackened. Ever resourceful, the group stained the others to match, and hung up fish nets to create an atmosphere. In the circumstances, rain at the first performance was a godsend. The enthusiasm of the steaming audience matched that of the players.

The acting might have ended there. All agreed that it had transformed the summer, but it was now time to go back to New York. Jig could not let the matter rest. He stayed up later than the others and almost every day he would go over to the wharf and open the sliding door in the black wall which commanded a view of the harbor and the low hills of Truro over the bay. Over and over again he paced out the dimensions, calculating the size of a possible stage and how to vary it so that the experimental plays he sought could get their proper setting. He told Susan that mere creation on paper was not enough for him. He had to organize a group and to shape things with his hands. The carpentry which the little wharfhouse would need was as satisfying to him fundamentally as *Change Your Style.*

That winter he would not let people alone. He was forever harping on the subject of drama. Jig Cook knew the Hell-Hole, in the back of which the Hudson Dusters and their friend Eugene O'Neill would often sit. Since Jig talked everywhere, the chances are the Hudson Dusters could have learned if they had cared to how true drama is born of the spirit which animates a group. It seems quite likely that Eugene avoided such conversations because they bored him. He was not a theorist, and anyway drink for the moment was more important. But Jack Reed, who had known Eugene since shortly after he left Princeton, was afire with enthusiasm, describing a miracle play he had seen in Mexico which had been performed in unbroken tradition for unnumbered years. Unquestionably, O'Neill did hear what Jig Cook was planning, and he must have wondered about it.

The Provincetowners, welded together by their summer experience, had formed a Village group whose peculiar madness centered around Jig Cook. He could think of nothing but what they must carry out the following summer.

In 1916, Cook was back in Provincetown early to begin work on the theater. From somewhere or other he had acquired a little money for lumber. Mary Vorse had contributed an old stage curtain which her family had rigged up in their attic at Amherst for children's theatricals. Jig got the boat out at last and restored the rest of the junk to its proper owners. He made more durable, though backless, benches. His main efforts, however, were concentrated on the stage. He planned it ten feet by twelve and built in four sections so that plays could be on different levels. They could even run the platforms out through the big sliding door, or simply leave this open and play against a background of sea and stars.

This year they were going to be much more ambitious. They would charge a small admission and use the money to make props. An evening's entertainment was going to be a full one. That is to say, three one-act plays would take the place of the usual three-acter. They did not consider anything longer, partly because rehearsals of small plays were comparatively simple, partly because the staging needed was simpler, too; but chiefly because none of them felt competent to construct anything larger.

They had a few plays to begin with. John Reed, who had been away in Mexico the previous summer, was enthusiastic and had written a piece called *Freedom*. Neith Boyce had produced another play. Susan Glaspell had not, but *Suppressed Desires* was considered well worth a second performance. These three plays, then, made up an evening's bill and were received with as much enthusiasm as ever. When one realizes that great successes of the period on Broadway were entitled *Twin Beds* and *Peg o' My Heart*, one can understand this.

No sooner was the evening over than planning began for the next. Wilbur Daniel Steele had written *Not Smart*, a little comedy dealing with marital relations complicated by misunderstandings between Villagers and native Provincetowners. Louise Bryant, a brilliant and attractive girl from Oregon who was known to be Jack Reed's girl, had written *The Game*. So far, so good, but they were ambitious to broaden themselves. They had in reserve three plays they had performed the year before, but one of these was by Steele, already on the program. The others were by Cook and Boyce, represented on the preceding bill. Unless they wanted to be known as a small, tight clique, they must draw in someone else.

They had done a great deal of talking the preceding winter. Indeed, one gets the impression that Polly's and the Liberal Club had rung with arguments on drama. The fact is, however, that there was much else to discuss. World War I was dragging on. The disastrous campaign of the British on Gallipoli had taken place, and the awesome victories of Hindenburg and Ludendorff over the Russians had been won. America was getting more deeply involved against her will. *The Masses* was loudly campaigning against war. But the influence of the world crisis was being felt. That splendid optimism with which the Village had started out on its erratic way was tarnished now. It was sadly evident that human nature was not so easily reformed as people had assumed.

The real struggle which was being fought out inside the Village that winter was not concerned with the future of plays in Provincetown. It was the struggle of the individualist for a faith that would help him in increasingly troubled times. The exhilaration of being simply oneself had worn off, yet the creative artist was by no means willing to go back home and settle into the life he had abandoned. He had to press on and find something else which would give him a sense of community again. The world had proved too vast for him to move it alone. He needed a common cause.

Two causes were to present themselves: the faith of Jig Cook in the creative spirit, and that of John Reed in social revolution. Jig Cook found his inspiration in his Players and in the genius of O'Neill. John Reed found his in the victory of Lenin in Russia. But in 1916, Czarist Russia still struggled, though in terrible agony. Jig's theater could hardly yet be said to exist. He was not conscious of O'Neill. Thus neither alternative was really yet presented to the imagination of the Village. Many other ideas occurred and seemed important. In such a time of searching, there was more talk than ever. Jig's did have an impact, but less than might have been supposed. He did not meet the problems of the age head on, as many felt impelled to.

All this may partly explain why Cook had not inspired the writing of more plays, especially when one considers the ferment of the preceding year or two. In addition, the life of the Village was apt to revolve around one's usual table at Polly's, one's preference for the Hell-Hole over O'Connor's, or one's habit of visiting Romany Marie's in the early hours of the morning. The Provincetowners had fallen into a way of life which brought them into one another's company. Their interests were not, perhaps, as widely diffused as might be expected.

The difficulty of the Provincetowners in 1916 was a real one. They needed O'Neill as badly as he needed them.

His sudden arrival with exactly the sort of play they had in mind was saluted by Jig as a proof of his theory. "If the right theatrical group is founded," Jig always said, "plays will be written." Actually this was not quite true of *Bound East for Cardiff*, which had been shown to Baker at Harvard before the Provincetown Players were ever thought of. All the same, the play had been called out of its hiding place by the existence of the Provincetown group. Before too long, the inspiration the Players provided was to bring forth new O'Neills.

Bound East for Cardiff is a one-act play with very little action. In the forecastle of the *S.S. Glencairn* Yank lies dying from an accidental fall. Around him the life of the ship is going on as his mates tumble out to go on watch or come back down. They are sorry and a little awed, but only Driscoll really cares. With him Yank talks of times they have had and plans he has made for their future together. The nearness of death lends him an eloquence which he clearly has never possessed before. Presently he dies, and that is all. Nothing could be more unlike Jig's little comedies on Village ideas or the satires on contemporary life and marriage which formed the bulk of productions among the Provincetown Players or in the Washington Square Theater. O'Neill was not portraying the clever, but the simple. His characters were unlettered men who worked with their hands. He was writing about them because he had lived among them and knew them well. If a point of view like O'Neill's was not unknown in European drama, here it was unique.

Among the group who heard the reading at Susan

Glaspell's, enthusiasm was immediate. Jig Cook had been waiting for drama to grow up out of the life of the people in his time. Before his eyes it had done so, and he recognized the fact. His ambition soared, and he was hopeful that he could elicit other important talents. Meanwhile, however, he burned to develop O'Neill's.

7 THE PROVINCETOWN GOES TO NEW YORK

TIDE WAS IN for the first performance of *Bound East for Cardiff*. Waves gurgled round the piers of the old wharf and washed occasionally through the holes which had swallowed umbrellas on that first opening night. There was fog out in the bay, and a bell punctuated the scene on the *S.S. Glencairn* with regular strokes. No better background could have been devised for the simple sentiment of the dying Yank, the fo'c'sle scene, the plebian language in which the characters expressed emotion.

Bound East for Cardiff is a study in contrasts. The crowded, unromantic quarters of the *S.S. Glencairn* are opposed to the vastness of the sea—the simplicity of the crew to the all-embracing mystery of death. No less effective was the contrast between O'Neill's work and the other two plays on the same bill. *Not Smart* by Steele was an uninspired example of the clever little comedies centering on marital relations which were the mainstay of the Provincetowners. *The Game* by Louise Bryant was another common type, a highly symbolic morality play in which Life and Death are playing dice while Youth and Girl look on. Set against these, *Bound East for Cardiff* had a raw immediacy.

Jig Cook, recognizing its quality, spurred the group on to a greater effort. Everything depended on Jig. Other people got bored, had to finish a story or a picture, rushed off to New York. Jig smoothed over arguments, settled problems, kept people coming to rehearsals. His help was needed over endless bits of carpentry or quests for objects which could be used on-stage. He had to rehearse the scene-shifting crew or wrestle with the dangers of lighting by oil lamps. In fact, he found work for all and kept them at it. In addition, he took his fair share of roles, including that of Yank in *Bound East for Cardiff*. He personally raised the necessary money; for though their most expensive set cost thirteen dollars, they had nothing to spare. He exhorted his friends to write more plays, but only John Reed obliged him. Jig had been selling subscriptions under the terms of which he was bound to produce two more bills. He turned on Susan:

"Now, Susan, I have announced a play of yours for the next bill."

Susan was horrified. "But I have no play."

"Then you will have to sit down tomorrow and begin one."

She protested vehemently. She had given shape to Jig's ideas in *Suppressed Desires,* but he had supplied the technical knowledge. By herself, she felt helpless. She had not studied playwriting. She did not know how to begin. Jig brushed these arguments aside.

"Nonsense!" he said in his sweeping way. "You've got a stage, haven't you?"

Poor Susan went over to the wharfhouse and sat on one of the backless benches by herself, staring at the stage. Pretty soon she began to think of the scene as a kitchen. People who write short stories usually have a number of half-complete ideas in their heads. The one which now possessed Susan stemmed from an old memory. She had been a reporter on an Iowa newspaper and had been sent down state to write up a murder trial. In the course of doing so, she went into the farmhouse where the tragedy had taken place. It gave her a queer feeling to see all the little daily things left just where they had lain when their owner was arrested.

Out of this conception *Trifles* was born. It is perhaps Susan Glaspell's best work, and certainly her best-known one. A farmer has been strangled while asleep in bed at night. His wife, in the same bed with him, claims she did not wake up. This seems incredible, and she has been arrested for murder. When the scene opens, the sheriff and district attorney have come to go through the house, looking for clues which may explain what has happened. The sheriff brings his wife and a local woman, in order that they may collect some clothes and other things the prisoner might need. The men find nothing. The women, who know how a housewife works and what little things are unusual, piece together the woman's story and her motive. She has done the deed, driven to it by her husband's tyranny. Torn between compassion and her duty to her own husband, the sheriff's wife decides in the end to hold her tongue.

Trifles is a model one-act play, a more beautiful piece of construction than O'Neill aspires to. The unraveling of the mystery gives suspense, which is heightened by the dilemma of the sheriff's wife. The tragedy outlined is sufficiently subtle to give distinction to the plot, while the sentiment so characteristic of Susan is here not out of proportion. The presence of *Trifles* on the third bill was a triumph for Jig. O'Neill, after all, was a piece of luck. *Bound East for Cardiff* was attracted, not inspired by the Provincetown Players. Susan's dramatic talent would not have displayed itself without her husband.

All the same, the two new playwrights were in violent contrast. *Trifles* is exactly like its name. It is a short story effectively cast into dramatic form. It is a one-act play which could not be made longer. *Bound East for Cardiff* is a lump of rock broken clumsily off a larger piece by sledgehammer action. Susan Glaspell has a neat idea tying all together. Women, she tells us, are more sensitive to subtleties than men. Eugene O'Neill has no neat ideas. He presents an episode out of human life without comment. No wonder Professor Baker dismissed *Bound East* as not really a play. Yet there is never any question about which of these two shows original talent.

The emergence of Susan Glaspell as a playwright benefited no one so much as O'Neill. It was hardly probable that the Provincetown Players would immediately discover a second dramatist with a genius to match his own. Indeed, such competition might not have been entirely welcome. But without some other talent, the Players must soon have foundered. They could not star O'Neill in every performance, while he had no other play in his present repertoire which was comparable to *Bound East for Cardiff*. As it was, Susan Glaspell's success kept enthusiasm going. *Trifles* made the fortune of the third bill. A revival of *Constancy* and a new play of Reed's were not distinguished, but one good original play in a bill was not a bad average.

In the last bill of the season, the Players produced two more revivals and a melodramatic, overwritten play of O'Neill's. *Thirst* presents a gentleman, a dancer, and a West Indian sailor adrift in an open boat without hope of rescue. The play is not truly realistic, and yet not symbolic either. *Thirst* was a failure, never repeated. All the same, it stands out against its fellow-plays on the program with a strong individuality. *Thirst* is the struggle between human beings obsessed by a need, a fate, a force outside themselves. It has the eternal theme of *Fog*, *Bound East for Cardiff*, and many later plays. A drama of such force could not be utterly ignored or even compared to its detriment with *Trifles*. No success of Susan Glaspell's could draw the attention of an audience from O'Neill.

A second remarkable thing about *Thirst* was that O'Neill himself acted the sailor, a taciturn character who does not say much except, "I have no water." He had also consented to walk on with a couple of lines in Reed's play on the preceding bill. Considering he hated acting and suffered from stage fright, his share in the Provincetown productions is a remarkable proof of his enthusiasm. The Players had transformed his world. He had an audience.

Terry Carlin and he had moved into a Provincetown shack, one of the old fishhouses. In their usual casual way they lived out of cans and threw the debris out of doors. O'Neill nailed a sign to the front door: "Go to Hell!" He did not want visitors while he was working, and he could have all the social life he needed among the Players. Across the road lay the house of Jack Reed, which was always full of guests and had Hippolyte Havel for a cook. But even when he joined in social gatherings, Eugene hardly spoke. He preferred to listen in silence, looking gloomy. Only occasionally would he talk on a subject which made him feel strongly. Then it was difficult to stop him. He would carry on through all interruptions in his low, hesitating voice, like a clockwork mechanism which has to run down.

Every day he would come out of his shack and stand in the sunlight, motionless, leaning against his back door, and gazing out to sea. After long minutes, sometimes even after hours, he would wade into the water and start swimming, straight out until he was almost invisible from land. When he emerged he was often joined by Louise Bryant, who was one of those who worried about these solitary swims. For the most part the two sat together on the beach, saying little or nothing. The situation somewhat scandalized even the free and easy Provincetowners, since Louise was Jack Reed's girl.

Eugene had met Louise in the preceding winter; and while Jack Reed was in Mexico, he had seen a good deal of her. It would not be fair to say he pursued her; it was rather that she did not let him alone. He could not, however, resist her attractions, even though John Reed was his friend. He suffered, while Louise relentlessly dug her claws into both men. Eventually, after long and public indecision, she married Reed and went to Russia with him, leaving Eugene to parade a broken heart. That was still in the future. In Provincetown, she exerted herself to break through his shell.

Behind the "Go to Hell!" sign, Eugene was trying intermittently to work. He was drinking in short bursts. The Provincetowners did not regard themselves as a drinking set and perhaps were drinking less than they normally did in New York, where they met in restaurants or bars. However, a couple of people had barrels of beer, and those who went down to New York would bring back bottles. Possession of whisky certainly meant one gave a party. With George Cook at least, talking and drinking went together. He was a large man and had large appetites. Terry Carlin had endless ingenuity in finding liquor. All in all, it was not too hard to get drunk fairly often; and the temptation was particularly strong for a shy man pitchforked into the middle of an intimate group. The

Provincetowners were soon aware of Eugene's alcoholic habits, but it was not their custom to criticize other people for their behavior. They left Eugene to struggle with himself.

He really was fighting over the matter. Drink and work did not go together. He wanted his head clear. How else could he direct his plays, observe their impact on his audience, discover how to make the best effect? Jig Cook was anxious for experiments, and there was nothing that O'Neill could not try out if he wanted to.

For all his indifference to commercial values, O'Neill was never above pleasing an intelligent audience. He was too practical a theater man. The purpose of drama is to hold an audience spellbound. The purpose of expressing ideas is to get them across. Eugene was not naturally eloquent, while the things he had to say were vast and imprecise. It was of the utmost importance that he study dramatic techniques. The Provincetown Players enabled him to learn by doing.

Jig Cook was becoming exalted. Everything that he had prophesied was coming true. Group spirit was high, and he had discovered talent. His enthusiasm soared beyond restraint. It was time to take the Players to New York.

Jack Reed encouraged this ambition; but Jack was an adventurer, always ready for a dare. Besides, he was already a success. Jack had tried his hand at a number of things, almost as various as the attempts of Jig Cook. The difference was, he had done fairly well with them all, while his recent exploits of reporting in Mexico had won him real fame as a foreign correspondent. In other words, Jack could toss off a failure. George Cook was more vulnerable. It seemed only too probable that New York would laugh. Provincetown acting was still amateurish. Settings might command the services of unconventional artists, but they had to be simple and cheap. The wharfhouse, primitive as it might be, was a better theater than they were likely to afford in New York. They would be offering a direct challenge to the Washington Square Theater with its decent facilities and financial backing.

These considerations did not weigh with Jig Cook. When he worked himself into one of these moods, he was impossible to control. He got the group together, twenty-nine of them by now, and persuaded them to draw up a statement of association. They would call themselves the Provincetown Players, and they would find a place to put on plays in New York. Almost everyone expected to name this the Provincetown Theater, which did in fact remain its popular title. O'Neill, however, had other ideas. He wanted it called The Playwright's Theater. In fact, he insisted on the name so strongly that the others had to give way. The trouble he took to gain this trivial point is a symptom of the importance to him of certain ideas.

The Playwright's Theater was to give dramatists a chance to experiment. Each should produce his own play, thus giving it the form that he desired. Every member of the group must write or act or work behind the scenes. To realize O'Neill's plans and Jig's glorious vision of a native American drama, eight people contributed thirty dollars apiece. The summer season had netted eighty dollars, which they had in hand. With this magnificent sum in his pocket, Jig Cook boarded a train for New York to find a theater in which to teach America to create drama. He did not forget to pop his head out of the train and shout to Susan, "Write another play!"

He found on old brownstone not far from the Liberal Club and Polly Halliday. Number 139 Macdougal Street had a couple of large rooms on the ground floor, divided by sliding doors which would do for a curtain. It was not much of a place. Rough carpentry could make a stage. Seats in the parlor might be built up in tiers. The benches would be difficult to climb into and uncomfortable, but they would seat a hundred and fifty. It was daunting to discover that a steel beam would have to be installed to bear this weight, and that it would cost a couple of hundred dollars. But Jig was not to be put off by mere lack of money. He took everyone into his confidence; the landlady, the electrician, the real-estate man, the policeman, and even the city building inspector, who shook his head. The very garbage collectors were made sharers in Jig's dream.

The iron beam was duly installed and the seats were built. It then became obvious that the sliding doors would not do. An architect friend undertook to rip out the partition and insert two beams, but the building department would not agree. Jig and his friends were not to be put off. They did the work secretly one Sunday and carted away the debris by night. The inspector, however, came round again a few weeks later; and he took them to court. Ida Rauh, who had had legal training, argued the case. The judge dismissed it.

There were not many amenities at 139 Macdougal Street, in spite of these efforts. The single dressing room was upstairs. Men managed more or less behind a screen, while ladies retired one at a time into a remodeled corner closet. The only way of getting on-stage was to tiptoe down the stairs and through the hall while the audience was not looking. The stage itself was inadequate for the shifting of scenery and the storing of props, save with the utmost care in managing both. Jig had to spend endless time working out arrangements.

In the late fall of 1916, the Provincetown Players opened, announcing three one-act plays to a bill, three performances a week, and a run of two weeks for each bill. As a start, they put their best foot forward with *Bound East for Cardiff.*

In one sense, Jig's venture justified itself immediately. In the larger society of the Village, far more new plays were available. Indeed, in that first winter, the Players produced eight bills with twenty-four plays, only four of which were revivals. Over half the new ones were written by people who had not previously been associated with the group. In addition, four of the eight bills contained plays by O'Neill, all except *Bound East for Cardiff* being new to the public.

By no means were all twenty new plays worth much trouble, but Jig always gave of his best. It was his conviction that the fumbling playwright needed a production.

How else could he learn? Michael Gold, whose *Ivan's Homecoming* was on the seventh bill, was at the time an assistant truck driver for an express company. He brought a play to Jig, who glanced through it and began to talk to its author about what he intended. In fact, Jig read so much into the work that, "He made me," Gold exclaimed, "feel like a god." It was a sensation which Jig was able to give to other young playwrights.

O'Neill was experimenting as well as the rest. His last stage role, if one can call it that, was the husband in his own *Before Breakfast*. The play is a monologue by a nagging wife who screams at her husband as he gets up and dresses off-stage. His only appearance consists in stretching out an arm for the hot shaving water which she has ready for him. Eventually, still off-stage, he uses the razor to cut his throat with a realistic gurgle. How long can such a monologue go on without the audience becoming restive? In what ways can the monotony be varied? O'Neill was testing out the matter. Monologues in many of his later plays profit from his observations.

There were no reserved seats and no free tickets offered to dramatic critics in the Playwright's Theater. Since some of the Players had newspaper connections, a few critics occasionally found their way downtown. Nothing was made easy for them. There was no telephone and no box office. Frank Shay, who had bought Boni's bookshop, did sell tickets, if one knew the fact or could get hold of him. The arrangement worked more or less in the Village, where everybody knew everybody else. In the larger area of New York, it presented problems.

Such critics as appeared downtown were not unimpressed. If the average quality of plays was not very high, it was also not low. Intelligent people were writing about their own times and had fresh things to say. The productions might rely heavily for costumes on the second-hand clothes shop down the street, but they were obstinately experimental. Floyd Dell complains that the Provincetowners produced a play of his on stilts and that when the group bought a wind machine, Jig drowned every possible production in the roar of a mechanical blast. Maybe so, but the Playwright's Theater had vitality. Since only those critics who cared about drama took the trouble to appear, they were willing to notice the merits of the Players. The sets, they concluded, were childlishly primitive. The acting was amateurish. The plays, however, were intelligent and at their best impressive.

Bound East for Cardiff was the only O'Neill production which deserved this cautious praise. *Fog* and *Thirst*, though interesting, were certainly failures. *The Sniper*, an out-of-date war play written at Harvard, was hardly even characteristic. The truth was, all these had come out of the trunkful which Terry had mentioned to Susan. Since joining the Players, Eugene had completed nothing save the little experiment, *Before Breakfast*.

The trouble was, he could not concentrate. He was never an author who could work between social engagements. He needed solitude. At the moment, his love affair with Louise Bryant was running its hectic course. He was directing his own plays, immensely particular about details of acting and production. He was even, as we have seen, taking minor roles himself. The atmosphere of the Village, meanwhile, was impossible for him. It abounded in places in which he had been drinking the preceding winter. He had parted with Terry Carlin, it is true, and had been offered quarters in the apartment of a friend. But the barman at one of his father's favorite hotels was generous with credit. Old friends at the Hell-Hole welcomed his return. His new companions drank freely if not dangerously. There was everywhere temptation for a man who could not resist a drink or stop drinking once he had started.

Early in 1917, he fled to Provincetown. As though he had stored it up all winter, work came pouring forth. In a few weeks he had finished four one-act plays, all far superior to the rejects to which the Provincetowners had been reduced. The O'Neill plays of their second New York season would soon prove how enormously production had benefited his work. *The Long Voyage Home, Ile* and *The Rope* have unmistakable power. In the first of these a sailor who longs to end his wanderings and settle down is shanghaied in a bar and shipped back to sea. The fate which dominates his life is not so easily to be shaken off. *Ile* is based on a Provincetown story told Eugene by Mary Vorse. A whaling captain who has not yet filled his barrels refuses to turn home. His crew is near mutiny and his wife is going out of her mind, but an obsession grips him. *The Rope* is a grim story of an angry father and a covetous son. All three concern themselves with man as the prisoner of forces, either inner or external, which he cannot control. In *Fog* and *Thirst* the characters were types, so that in-

117

terest was focused on typical reactions. The struggle of the captain with his obsession in *Ile,* of the father and son in *Rope,* even the pathetic attempt of destiny's victim to escape in *The Long Voyage Home* are tragedies of individuals. O'Neill is exploring the human heart, and his master now is Freud.

Enthusiasm had carried the Playwright's Theater through one season and launched it on the next. Jack Reed had persuaded the New York Stage Society to buy some tickets. Frank Shay, the Boni brothers' successor, published *The Provincetown Plays* in a series of little pamphlets which had no great sale but did spread the knowledge of what Jig was doing. Financially the Players picked up money where they could. Clubs asked the group for speakers. On its empty nights, the little theater could be hired for dance recitals, concerts, and the like. The Liberal Club was willing to rent its theatrical props for five dollars an evening when not in use. When the season of 1917–18 opened, The Provincetown was secure in its modest place. In this second year, it increased its performances to five a week, and lengthened its runs to three weeks, proof of how rapidly its audience was increasing.

The year 1917 was a curious one in which to be running an amateur theater. America had gone to war. Greenwich Village was deeply disturbed by World War I, of which few Villagers approved. Used to thinking for themselves, they were not in tune with public sentiment. They had always condemned both sides alike, and they continued to do so. All the same, they felt their isolation.

118

Their dam had broken, and the waters of chaos were rising about them. Floyd Dell, Max Eastman, and *The Masses* in general ignored the feeling of the times and kept on publishing their anti-war propaganda. John Reed, returning briefly from Russia, was more vehement. He had been covering the spectacular events which had made Lenin master of Russia. His own rebellious temperament had led him to communism.

The group which formed the nucleus of the Provincetown Players was concerned with other values. Immersed in his private struggle with Fate, O'Neill cared little for political events. In fact, his chief preoccupation in 1917 was to avoid the draft. He applied for a doctor's certificate on account of his tuberculosis, but was turned down. He spent most of his summer in New London near his draft board, where he quarreled interminably with his father. James disapproved of his anti-war attitude. He disapproved also of his resolute refusal to earn. All the preceding winter, Eugene had subsisted on James's allowance of a dollar a day. He could have had free quarters with his father, but refused them. With the help of friends and by sharing a room he had managed, but the difficulty had contributed to his nonproductive period. Disputes between the father and son now raged daily. Eugene, of course, got drunk. Eventually he wore his father down. In August, James made it possible for him to go back to Provincetown.

He, Terry, and another friend moved into a little apartment above a general store on Commercial Street. Their landlord, John Francis, was the kindest man in town. He never collected his rent because the tenants were so obviously hard up. He even extended credit for groceries. James had arranged for meals at a local hotel, but these were mostly taken out in liquor. However, Eugene and his friends were anxious not to impose too heavily on Francis, and they lived almost entirely on oatmeal.

Bronzed from hours on the beach and as yet untapped by his draft board, Eugene came back to the Village in the fall of 1917, bringing with him his little pile of plays. He had even sent copies of some to a literary magazine called *The Smart Set*, which published *The Long Voyage Home* and paid him for it. He was beginning, in fact, to make his way.

Jig Cook was still full of enthusiasm. Mainly because of the improvement in O'Neill's plays, the second season for the Provincetowners went better than the first. Other playwrights, however, were growing up too. Susan Glaspell might be content with easier answers to smaller questions, but she had a deft hand with comedy and could write more serious works as well. *The Outside*, a woman's struggle with loneliness, is given poetic values by being related to the desolate sand dunes which Susan had learned to love in Provincetown.

Jig Cook himself was no less sure than O'Neill that World War I was an interruption of things more important and lasting. He could not help comparing the situation in 1917 with that of Athenian drama and the conditions which had brought it forth. He remembered how war had dulled the glorious spirit of Athenian theatre. The age of

Pericles had turned sour. The age of American drama had hardly begun, and yet already the war was distorting men's values. Jig was anxious lest his vision fade. He felt the necessity of expressing his convictions, but his message was by no means that of John Reed or of *The Masses*. He aspired to be a prophet, not a reformer. Jig's ambitions at this point had a personal side. He had been too busy discovering dramatists to become one. Yet his faith in his creative abilities had been revived by a taste of success. It was not enough for him to have found a Euripides. He must become Sophocles himself.

Why not? So far the Provincetowners had stuck to their repertoire of one-act plays. Sooner or later they must aspire to full-length drama or lose their O'Neills and possibly even their Glaspells. Always perceptive where his theater was concerned, Jig felt he ought to lead the way. His preoccupation with ancient Greece provided a theme and a model. Aristophanes' *Lysistrata* is a witty burlesque in which the women of Athens refuse to put up with war. Domestically they are potent enough to make their men see reason. Why not solidify *Lysistrata* by bringing in Pericles himself and the famous characters of the Greek golden age? Let it be a drama of values, not an irreverent, if bitter comedy. Let it show what are the fruits of war.

The Athenian Women, produced in March, 1918, was the Players' first long play, not entirely a failure, yet certainly not a success. It is unfortunately less good than the *Lysistrata*. In fact, it is loaded with well-intentioned learning. Aristophanes could be flippant about the extraordinary people of his time. He and his audience could take for granted the society in which they moved. Re-creating it for modern times, Cook must treat its famous figures more seriously. This is a difficulty which has ruined many a would-be masterpiece on the golden age of Athens.

In 1918, despite the steady advance of the Province-towners, the group began to bog down. This was partly due to the effort of staging Jig's play with its thirty charac-ters. It was partly the distractions of war, the wearing off of enthusiasm, and the necessity of meeting higher stand-ards as the little theater became noticed. There was a feel-ing that Jig Cook was almost a nuisance. Nothing could be done without him, and yet he could not be in every spot at once. Criticism mounted. For a period, it looked as though the Players were falling apart. They were saved by the very thing Jig had always relied on. They acted as a focus for new talent. Somebody with professional experi-ence in producing plays was needed. In the nick of time, somebody came. The business correspondence, the errands, finances, publicity, tickets found a competent handler in Eleanor Fitzgerald, who from this time devoted her life to the Provincetown. As new recruits brought fresh enthusi-asm, things improved. The subscription audience climbed to nine hundred. An occasional and favorable review ap-peared in the papers.

The third bill of the 1917–18 season had opened with a Floyd Dell comedy entitled *The Angel Intrudes*. An angel, straying down to earth and adopting human costume, appears to a romantic couple. He is susceptible to the lady's charm. She soon forsakes her lover for the new attraction. The cast was being made up when a little redhead in her early twenties appeared to try out for the girl. She proved to have a deep and expressive voice which won her the part.

"What is your name?" Jig was making notes.

"Millay."

He started to write it down, when a thought came to him. He stared at her. "Not the girl who wrote *Renascence?*"

She nodded.

In this way a second original talent appeared among the Provincetowners.

In 1912, a middle-aged practical nurse in Maine went out on a case. She was supporting three daughters, the eldest of whom had already graduated from high school and was at loose ends. In an idle moment, Mrs. Millay picked up a magazine which someone had tossed into the wastebasket and leafed through it. Her eye fell on an announcement that a collection of original lyrics by American authors was planned. There was a deadline for sending poems in and a prize of five hundred dollars. She clipped the story out for her eldest daughter, Vincent.

Ferdinand Pinney Earle, who was the moving spirit in this venture, had not reckoned with the swelling tide of American verse. He had expected a few hundred poems, and he got ten thousand. He settled grimly down with a friend to sort them out. A good many were fit for nothing but the wastebasket. Occasionally one or other of them would groan and read aloud something especially bad.

All I could see from where I stood
Was three long mountains and a wood.
I turned and looked another way,
And saw three islands in a bay.

declaimed the friend in disgust. He tossed the manuscript away.

"That's not bad," protested Earle, his attention caught. He rescued the poem and read it through with growing excitement. Presently he dashed off a letter to Vincent Millay, telling her that she was sure to win the prize. He spoke too soon. There were three judges, and the others overruled him, preferring a poem of social protest by Orrick Johns. *Renascence* did appear in *The Lyric Year*, but it took only fourth place.

With one voice the critics wanted to know why. *Renascence*, they agreed, was the only poem which stood out. The injustice done it soon made it far more famous than it would have been had it won. Johns refused to attend the official dinner and presentation of his prize, on the grounds that he had not deserved to win.

Such a talent as Edna St. Vincent Millay's deserved the best education. Someone made it possible for her to go to Vassar. After graduation, she came to New York. She could hardly support herself by writing poetry, which almost never pays. She had hopes of becoming an actress. Broadway, however, was unimpressed. The Provincetowners offered experience. Edna St. Vincent Millay joined the

124

group and resigned herself, as Susan Glaspell did, to making her living by writing for magazines.

Like every new success of the Provincetown Players, the arrival of Miss Millay benefited O'Neill. Primarily a poet, she wrote only one masterpiece for the group. O'Neill remained its professional playwright, dedicated entirely to one form of art. It was true that his dramas were winning the Provincetown a reputation. It was equally obvious that the higher the quality of their other productions, the more critics would be aware of the latest O'Neill.

8 THE WHOLE WORLD'S HERE

IN THE SECOND SEASON of the Provincetown Players, Jig Cook had been offered a modest subsidy. Unhesitatingly he had seized his chance to weld the Players together by renting a second floor and installing a restaurant. He had long seen the necessity for a place where they could drop in between rehearsals to continue discussion as they ate. For a period Nani Bailey in Fourth Street had catered to them, but she presently went abroad. In any case, it would be better if they did not have to go outside the building. The trouble was that O'Neill preferred to slip down to the Hell-Hole for a quick one. Once he got started on a drink, he would not return. One of the men would go to fetch him and would not come back either. Eventually Jig would go in person. He would sit down to argue with the delinquents and presently would get absorbed. No further work would be done that afternoon.

This might have been possible with three performances a week; but with the five which Jig planned, it was a disaster. In 1917, therefore, the restaurant opened with Christine Ell in charge to feed the Players.

Christine Ell was a huge, voluptuous, red-haired woman whose face was at once hideous and striking. She was of Danish extraction and had been brought to the United States as an infant by her mother and stepfather. She had managed to break out of the slums by sheer force of character and had adopted anarchist views, which taught her that the degradation of her early life was not her fault, but that of society. Before setting up her own restaurant, she had held a job at Polly Halliday's, where she had made many friends. She was vivid, amusing, and a wonderful mimic. She was also tempestuous and slapdash. It is said that her premises were once fumigated, with the result that three pails of assorted cockroaches, mice, and other pests were gathered up. But she was a good cook and liked to consult the individual tastes of her customers. Her husband, Louis Ell, was carpenter and handyman to the Players, who soon gathered the couple into their circle. Their life together was punctuated by shattering rows, for Christine had a roving eye and Louis was jealous.

Christine had her Danish mother with her, and she installed her in a little room off the restaurant. The old lady was getting senile by now, and she had a strong disapproval of actors. She popped into the restaurant from time to time to tell the Players that they all came from the devil and would return to him. One day she emerged, clad only in long winter woolies, to pursue O'Neill with a meat cleaver for teaching Christine to read Nietzsche.

On the whole, there was plenty of drama at Christine's as well as in the theater. Dinners there cost sixty cents. On opening and closing nights there was a party. Punch was made in an aluminum pot from the kitchen; and Jig Cook, always at his best on festive occasions, made a little ceremony of dipping the first cupful. The parties were gay, occasionally wildly so. The Players brought their friends, so that many an interested person made his way up to Christine's and met the group. The Provincetowners were becoming a Village elite and were attracting increasingly distinguished notice.

The difficulties of producing *The Athenian Women* in 1918 had emphasized as never before the limitations of 139 Macdougal Street. Jig was on the lookout to expand, and one of his theater patrons actually offered him a thousand dollars for the purpose. He needed only to match it with another thousand. Between them he and Eleanor Fitzgerald managed it. What letters were written, what appeals were made, what pinching and scraping were needed, only he and "Fitzi" could have told. Their object was to move a few doors down the street. The house at 133 Macdougal was big and its upper floors still displayed remnants of grandeur. Its ground floor, on which Jig had his eye, had been used as a storehouse, a bottling works, and a stable. For these reasons, it had a sloping entrance ramp, out of which they could make a little lobby and actually a box office. Downstairs there was a basement, perfect for workshop and storeroom. They even boxed off one corner for their first real dressing rooms. In exuberance, the handyman painted over the entrance, "Cloze the door was you born in a stabel?" Seats were still backless benches, uncushioned, unnumbered, but the auditorium floor could be built into a ramp, thus reducing the perils of climbing into seats.

The group flung itself into the task of conversion in its usual resourceful spirit. There was a hitching ring left in the wall from old stable days. They polished it and put an inscription underneath, "Here Pegasus was hitched." The big front door, which was squeaky, had a tendency to swing open. Albert and Henry, aged eight and ten, were employed to lean against it for the sum of a quarter an evening. Presently the Players had time to fix the door, but by now they were fond of Albert and Henry. The boys kept their job, and Henry even brought in his brother when he got too old himself to work for a quarter.

They opened at 133 Macdougal Street in the fall of 1918 with Edna St. Vincent Millay's *The Princess Marries the Page*. This is a childish work which she had already put in shape for a performance at Vassar. It is pretty, but hardly a play for an experimental theater which had already turned down O'Neill's *In the Zone* as too conventional. Truth was, no doubt, that Miss Millay's name looked impressive on the program, while Jig may have wished to encourage her dramatic talent. In any case, her play was a mere curtain-raiser to O'Neill's *Where the Cross Is Made.* O'Neill by this time was becoming known.

He had made a hit the year before by *In the Zone,* produced by the Washington Square Players. This is a conventional and sentimental drama, using once more the crew of *S.S. Glencairn.* In the long run, O'Neill himself thought little of it; but it was good theater and took war tension as its theme. In the spring of 1918, he got an offer to take *In the Zone* on the vaudeville circuit—two hundred dollars in advance and seventy dollars a week. It ran thirty-four weeks, and Eugene considered himself incredibly rich. He used the money to get married.

In the second season at 139, he had been in New York to see to the details of production of his plays. He was proclaiming to all and sundry that his heart was broken on account of Louise, now married to Reed and gone to Russia. Several ladies consented to hold his hand. There was something about Eugene's dark intensity which attracted girls. They were always around him, and in their company he relaxed somewhat. Notwithstanding, he continued to parade his love for Louise.

Agnes Boulton was the daughter of a portrait painter, a gentle, impractical man who had never made much money to provide for his wife and four daughters. Agnes had married early, but her husband had died, leaving her with an infant daughter and a farm in northern Connecticut. Agnes had established her family here, in the hope apparently that they could make a living from it. She herself, with her baby and a sister to help, had come to New York for the winter of 1916–17. She had some writing talent and had received encouragement from magazines. She stayed long enough to make acquaintance with Christine Ell and also to invite Harry Kemp, the hobo poet, and his wife to summer on the farm.

Fortified by their encouragement, she returned in the fall of 1917 to the attack. She had a hundred dollars, and someone had commissioned a story. Little Barbara, whom she had left with her parents, did not miss her, or so she was assured. Agnes was not a maternal woman. It was her intention to return to her family and child in the spring, but she never went back.

Christine by now had moved to the Provincetown, and it was inevitable that Agnes and Eugene should meet. It chanced that physically she bore a considerable resemblance to Louise Bryant. Several people noticed this, including Eugene, who courted her. She was soon in love with him, and managed, as it were, to assert her claim. Eugene, who was finding New York no more conducive to work than he had the preceding year, was constantly talking about getting back to Provincetown; yet he lingered. Eventually, when the pair admitted their love, Louise Bryant Reed complicated the situation by returning from Russia before her husband. She tried to assert her old dominance. Agnes wept. Eugene swayed back and forth. Finally rejecting Louise, he was committed to her rival. *In the Zone* produced some timely money, and they were married in April of 1918.

Not all of Eugene's friends were entirely happy about

this match, and their misgivings were in part justified. Eugene demanded much from a wife. She must be a passionate lover, a mother to him, and housekeeper, and secretary as well. She must be entirely devoted to him and his ideals. Agnes Boulton did not measure up to these standards. She was, to be sure, much in love and prepared to sacrifice her family and infant daughter. Eugene insisted that they two were their own little world, yet he did introduce her eventually to his father and mother. Agnes did not dare expose him to Barbara yet. The following winter, she persuaded Eugene to take a short working vacation from New York in her family home in New Jersey, which, owing to various financial transactions, was in her name. To her horror, she discovered on arriving ahead of Eugene that her family had found winter on the Connecticut farm too much and had moved down. She made it clear that Eugene was not to be troubled by her relations. The family had to move, and her father took a job in a local hardware store to pay rent. When Christmas came, Agnes did steal downtown for an hour or two to take Barbara a toy. Even Eugene, when he discovered the situation, inquired why she had not told him her family was in town. She had clearly been afraid to.

Although Agnes was prepared to go to such extreme lengths with her family, she could not change herself. She had little interest in the theater, and she never acquired much. Her own writing for the pulps was moderately successful and accounted at first for a useful part of their income. Agnes took the view that she had her career, as Gene had his. Not being a motherly woman, she was not a good housekeeper, either. She was easygoing and in a mild way social, so that she never understood how Eugene shrank from people. Nor could she cope with his ups and downs of temperament. The Provincetowners had brought purpose into Eugene's life by giving him something to work for. Until he joined them, it had been likely that he would drink himself to death. He was transformed by success, yet he had not given up liquor. He still used it as a periodical relaxation, and as a cushion against failure. Agnes had problems with Eugene which she could not completely understand.

Her initiation started early. They came down from Provincetown about two weeks after their marriage. *Beyond the Horizon*, Eugene's first satisfactory full-length play, had actually impressed a Broadway producer who was willing to take some chance in putting on plays that he liked. John Williams had staged Galsworthy and others, but *Beyond the Horizon* was a bold risk, even for him. In a rash moment he had paid five hundred dollars for an option on it. But when O'Neill appeared to talk over production, Williams had lost his nerve. He put Eugene off. The result was an episode which Agnes described in detail many years later.

It had been agreed that Jamie, who was at loose ends in town, should come up to Provincetown and share their quarters over John Francis's store. Agnes, who was already put in charge of practical arrangements, got the tickets and packed. Eugene put on his good suit for the journey. Jamie arrived, bearing a bottle. There was still some time to wait. The brothers started drinking. Eventually Agnes saw they would never make it, so she went down to Grand Central and changed their sleeper reservations to the following night.

Next morning, Eugene felt too sick to eat breakfast, and he asked Agnes to go into the bar downstairs and get him an eggnog with brandy. For all her attempts at sophistication, Agnes had never before been alone in a bar. She did not like the experience, but after a few more days she got used to it. She had to change the reservations again that day, and the next day, and the next. The spree lasted a week. Eventually Eugene, his hand shaking so that she had to get a barber in to shave him, his digestion so ruined that he could hardly keep anything down, was bundled into a taxi and thence onto the train. There were many such episodes. What makes this one remarkable is that Agnes did not put two and two together. Incurious about theatrical affairs, she does not seem to have considered her husband's disappointment. She attributes that lost week to Eugene's reluctance to face the long train ride and tedious wait at Fall River. No doubt that is how he explained it to her, but it seems strange that he should have convinced her.

There is another side to this episode besides the revelation of a barrier between these two. It argues strongly that the Provincetown did save O'Neill. In a sense, perhaps, it can only be true that he saved himself. Had he not insisted upon absolute soberness and complete concentration when he did his work, he could never have conquered alcohol. It is true that the very intensity with which he worked made him turn back to his old friend to relax the tension. But it was the urge to create which made him shake off the habit time and again. It was encouragement, however, which made him work. From the time of the first production of *Bound East for Cardiff*, there were people about him convinced he had genius. With further productions, O'Neill's fame began to spread like a ripple through water, and he could see it widen.

Actually *Where the Cross Is Made* and *The Moon of the Caribbees* did little to help him for the moment. The first was frankly experimental, so much so that the Provincetowners worried about it. The move to the new theater had cost so much that Jig Cook gave a month's rent to the treasury and moved his bed on-stage. It was necessary that they get some of their outlay back. Some of the group, including Ida Rauh, who was directing, pointed out that three drowned ghosts appearing to two madmen are hard to make plausible on a stage only twelve feet deep and with the front benches of the audience twelve feet away. It would be simpler if the two madmen, not the audience, saw the ghosts. O'Neill, however, never took kindly to criticism. He insisted he was trying to send the audience mad along with the characters, and he wanted to know how far this could be done. The play was performed as he demanded.

The Moon of the Caribbees, which appeared on the second bill, has since been recognized as an outstanding one-act play. At the time it caused small sensation, possibly because O'Neill had once more strained the resources of the Provincetown stage in order to produce it. It is clear, however, that his disappointment was minor. He had his heart set on the uptown production of *Beyond the Horizon*, which was still delayed.

O'Neill's growing absorption with bigger things was reflected in the affairs of the Provincetown. Their two new O'Neills had not been great successes, and they only managed three further new bills and three old ones. Jig and Susan had written *Tickless Time*, a triviality. More notably, Susan had accomplished a longer play. *Bernice* is neither bad nor especially good. It further suffers by comparison with her later *Alison's House* on a similar theme. The importance of *Bernice* is that it shows how the leading spirits of the Provincetown were pushing on together. First Cook, then O'Neill, and now Glaspell, as they found confidence, were moving away from the one-act play. It remained to be seen how this development would affect the Provincetown.

By the summer of 1919, Agnes O'Neill was pregnant and clearly nervous about it. Eugene had never shown any desire for children. His work satisfied his creative instinct. He had always spoken of their marriage as just the two of them together. Eugene, however, was not displeased. He had sufficient share of normal feelings to put a good face on the matter, though the additional responsibility weighed heavy on him. The person who was unfeignedly joyful was James O'Neill.

It was gradually becoming clear to James that his son amounted to something. The vaudeville run had certainly impressed him. He had occasionally poked his nose in at the Provincetown to Eugene's fury and had gone so far as to tell the wife in *Before Breakfast* how to act her lines in a stagy, florid fashion which his son put a stop to at once when his back was turned. He had inquired plaintively why Eugene always wrote such unpleasant plays. In fact, he had interfered with an anxiety both fatherly and touching, but utterly tactless. He was, however, beginning to be hopeful. He was ready to like Agnes, even though she was not Irish, and to see the marriage as a sign of Eugene's settling down. Now he was going to have his first grandchild. He had long dismissed Kathleen's son, little Eugene, from his mind, for there was nothing halfhearted about James's prejudices. In his jubilation in 1919, he did, almost for the first time, the right thing for Eugene. He bought him a house.

It had been established by now that Provincetown was a place where Eugene could work. It suited him because he loved the sea. However, the flat above John Francis's store was no more than a single room divided by a board partition. It was hardly the place for a writer with a baby. Besides, it was too social. Eugene wanted a place where people could not drop in. He had his eye on the ideal spot, the old Coast Guard station at Peaked Hill Bars. It was this which James now bought and gave to his son.

The Atlantic coast, from which Provincetown was divided by about three miles of sand dunes, was wild and desolate. There were Coast Guard stations along it, for it was dangerous. A deadly combination of current, prevailing winds, and shifting sand bars had widowed many a Provincetown wife in the great days of sail. Even now, despite reliable lights, wreckings and drownings were commonplace. The Coast Guard patrolled the outer beaches constantly, though sometimes in a winter's storm when entire sand dunes were lifted bodily and hurled through the air, men finished their tour on hands and knees. In such a place the sea was always encroaching or else being driven back. The Coast Guard station which watched over Peaked Hill Bars had been abandoned quite recently because the sea was coming too close for safety. Sooner or later in some winter storm it would wash away.

Meanwhile, in summers the place lay empty, overlooked only by the new Coast Guard station half a mile off. Mabel Dodge, the wealthy Greenwich Village hostess, had bought it as a summer place a few years back and fixed it up with considerable skill. It consisted mainly of one big room where lifeboats had been stored and, on many an occasion, corpses had been laid out. She had painted this gleaming white, upholstered her furniture in blue, and hung blue and green plates on the walls. She had made the place comfortable. Kerosene provided light and fuel. There was a big fireplace, too, and a gasoline pump for the water. Presently, however, she had taken a dislike to Provincetown. Accustomed to be queen, she did not fit readily into its informal atmosphere. She had also quarreled with Jack Reed about that perennial storm center, Louise Bryant. She put the place, just as it was, up for sale.

Eugene was absolutely delighted. On the second floor there was a lookout room entirely surrounded by windows, at which he could work in full view of the sea. He adored the sea's every mood and the constant sound of breakers. His favorite forms of exercise were swimming or paddling a kayak far out into dangerous waters in a way which amazed even the fishermen. At Peaked Hill Bars, he would not get visitors often. There was no road in, and the only way to reach him was to walk three miles over the dunes. He and Agnes either carried their own supplies or got a wagon drawn by old Daisy, the Coast Guard horse, to cart them.

It was not practical to stay here all year round. The place was not sufficiently heated, and storms were dangerous. As it was, every summer they had to have the windows re-glazed because flying sand had ground them until they were no longer transparent. That fall, the O'Neills moved into the village where, on October 30, 1919, Shane O'Neill was born.

While the O'Neills were waiting in Provincetown for this event, the Playwright's Theater was opening once more in New York, but without Jig Cook in charge. Several facts had contributed to this. Discontent with his management was rising. The Provincetown was now so settled an institution that it did not depend on his enthusiasm to keep going. Once this had been perceived, it also became apparent that Jig was not without faults. He had no idea of delegation and wanted to play all the instruments in the band. Nor was he in any sense a businessman. He had no system. He did things as they occurred to him. He worked endlessly, but knocked off when the impulse happened to strike him, and without consulting others. He was not by training a producer; and he brought to the task, some felt, more whimsicality than judgment. In short, all was not well inside the Provincetown. The situation was intensified because the Players had recently acquired a member with some of the qualities Jig lacked. James Light had come to New York to take a degree at Columbia and had happened to rent a room at 133 Macdougal Street, above the Provincetown. He had been immediately drawn in, had abandoned his degree, and proved his value among the younger members of the group.

Jig Cook himself was partly hurt but partly pleased. His ideal theater was growing up, and this was as it should be. Besides, he needed time to work. His dormant ambition had been roused by the production of *The Athenian Women*. He was conscious of other splendid ideas in his head. During the New York season he had no time to write. In the summers, there were too many distractions, and he needed a break. On the whole, Jig was content to stay in Provincetown all winter long. Let the younger group have its chance! He left it undecided whether he would return the following year. But he reserved the option.

The 1919–20 season opened with *The Dreamy Kid* at the Provincetown. This is a tale of a Negro gangster, and is generally considered one of O'Neill's minor plays. Socially, however, it made theatrical history. O'Neill had introduced Negro characters into several of his plays, but in minor roles. In *The Dreamy Kid* he paved the way for an understanding of the fact that the Negro's position as underdog in our society is not comic and has important social implications. Underlining this, Ida Rauh, the producer, insisted on hiring three Negro actors from a Harlem company. In *The Moon of the Caribbees,* in the preceding year, the Negro woman had been played by white actresses in dark make up. O'Neill himself had taken the role of the

Negro sailor in *Thirst*. It had never been the practice to hire Negroes for any parts save comic servants or vaudeville minstrels. *The Dreamy Kid* first introduced Negroes to the professional stage in a serious drama. But the success of *The Dreamy Kid* was social, not artistic. It made a sensation, but was not well reviewed. The high point of the season was Edna St. Vincent Millay's *Aria da Capo*, an immediate hit.

Miss Millay was never primarily a dramatist, and *Aria da Capo* is a tribute to Jig's view that if conditions are suitable to the writing of drama, talented people will produce it. The play is an outcry against the futility of war and the indifference of society to its evils. It manages to handle this extraordinarily large theme within the compass of a one-act play of great poetic charm. But though *Aria da Capo* made a sensation and deservedly enhanced Miss Millay's reputation, she planned no further play to follow it up. Thus her success was chiefly beneficial to the Provincetown and to O'Neill. Once more it was true that every production of merit brought fresh people to the theater where his works were chiefly performed. His audience was growing.

A striking proof of change in the public taste was soon afforded when *Beyond the Horizon* opened on Broadway in February, 1920. It was an inexpensive production got up by a company which was presenting another play. It was only given in a series of special matinees for the present. But the critics came, and the critics liked it. O'Neill's play was so different from Broadway's usual fare that they did not precisely know how to place it. But they were impressed. Something new had appeared on the American professional stage. They noted the fact, but did not imagine that *Beyond the Horizon* would ever be a hit. They were quite wrong.

Various explanations have been offered for the very real success of *Beyond the Horizon.* Perhaps the infiltration of serious European dramas had led the way. Perhaps a new postwar audience was inclined to take life seriously. O'Neill himself attributed it to the efforts of the Provincetown and the Washington Square Theater. They had, he said, created an atmosphere and an audience. He was possibly right. At all events, when *Beyond the Horizon* opened in Chicago, it proved to have no audience there as yet.

Eugene now tasted success. He earned far more money than he had ever done before and was awarded the Pulitzer Prize for *Horizon* in 1920. The Pulitzer Prizes in various creative fields had only been established three years before, and O'Neill had never heard of them. He now got a wire to say that the Board of Columbia University, which makes these awards, had chosen *Horizon* as the original American play of the year "best representing the educational value and power of the stage in raising the standard of good morals, good taste, and good manners."

This curious definition of the value of a play has always been interpreted in the broad sense of "artistically best" by Columbia. O'Neill, not unnaturally confused by the language, as well as by the notice of Columbia itself, jumped to the conclusion that the University was giving him some academic citation or medal. It would mean a ceremony and probably even a speech. He hastily prepared to turn it down. His agent, however, was more knowledgeable. He wasted no time in wiring O'Neill that the prize was a thousand dollars and that no ceremonies were attached. A thousand dollars! Eugene spent money as fast as it came in, and even *Horizon* had not yet made him solvent. He was overwhelmed. In fact, the Pulitzer, he later said, was about the most pleasant surprise of his whole life.

James O'Neill lived to hear of the Pulitzer award. He had attended the first night of his son's play with pride and had gloated over Eugene's success, just as though he had always believed in his future. On these terms, he and Eugene had a kind of reconciliation which was made happier because Ella's drug habit after all these years was really cured. She had insisted on going to a nunnery for some months instead of to a sanitarium. The experience had helped her. James's family was pleasanter than it had ever been, though Jamie, now apparently quite hopeless, was drinking more than ever. When the Pulitzer news came, James was dying of cancer; but he kept the telegram beside him and showed it to everyone. None could begrudge him this final triumph, for his death was hard.

The death of James O'Neill removed the powerful personality which had dominated his family for so long. The results were immediately felt. Relieved of his loving care and protection, Ella O'Neill displayed an unexpected business ability, which was much needed in straightening out the tangled results of his speculations. Jamie, more surprisingly still, gave up liquor to devote his whole time to his mother. His long war with James for her attention was over. He had it now and became a different man.

Eugene, who had already won his independence, was working intensively. Success had come to him, and he felt himself still at the beginning of his creative life. New ideas were plentiful. He was also reworking early plays in a different form. But Broadway, though interested in him now, was not receptive to the variety of his experiments. Managers wanted something as close to *Beyond the Horizon* as possible. O'Neill was offering *The Straw*, a play about a tuberculosis sanitarium which seemed dangerously crude, and *Gold*, a full-length version of *Where the Cross Is Made*, to which even the Provincetown Players had objected. He had in addition completed two plays which were neither full-length nor one-act, but in between. He was now considering something immensely long. All in all, he seemed to take no account of the problems of Broadway.

The situation was Jig Cook's opportunity. O'Neill offered him *The Emperor Jones*, considering it too experimental a play for Broadway production and too short. Once Jig had read it, nothing would have kept him up in Provincetown. He descended on New York in the fall of 1920, convinced that he held in his hands the future of the Provincetown Players. *The Emperor Jones* was to open the season, and everything else must give way to its production.

He had wanted a dome in the Provincetown stage for some time. This arrangement had been used with great success in the small art theaters of Europe as a device to reflect light and give an effect of distance. Wrestling with the problem of producing the illusion of sky and forest on his tiny stage, he now determined that, whether finances permitted or not, they must have that dome. It must be made of rough concrete so that it would not wrinkle or move, as a canvas dome might, and it would cost some three hundred and fifty dollars, presuming that the Players did most of the work. Once more Jig donated a month's rent to the cause and slept in the theater.

He barely got his way. The proposed expense was going to swallow almost every cent in the treasury, accumulated by careful cheeseparing over the past years. There were endless quarrels over Jig's extravagant ideas. Fitzi wrung her hands. Other people begged him to put off *The Emperor Jones* until the second bill or the third, by which time presumably subscriptions would have come in. He would not even discuss this. Time and again he walked out of a meeting, only to return, endlessly insisting, "We must do it!" Meanwhile none of the Players but Jig had seen the play, for O'Neill kept the manuscript in Provincetown and was in no haste to send it down.

Jig sacrificed eight feet of his precious stage, but he got his dome. No sooner was it in place than the Players came round to his view. The effect was spectacular. It really did give an illusion of distance on that small and cluttered stage. It was evident that the sets, already produced, would need to be redone. Cook discovered an engineer called Cleon Throckmorton and gave him the job. He proved to have great talent.

No one was sure later on who it was that insisted a Negro play the title role. It was difficult to get hold of one with sufficient experience. There was, however, a Negro actor called Charles Gilpin who had recently been playing a small part as a Negro slave in Drinkwater's *Abraham Lincoln.* Jig found him running an elevator and brought him down to read the script. He was chosen at once.

Mary Vorse, who came into the theater while Jig was coaching Gilpin for his role, long afterward recalled his marvelous courtesy and tact in a situation which was not particularly easy. Gilpin was touchy and suspected condescension, and yet his immense monologue required the most careful production. Jig's gifts as a teacher, which were perhaps his most genuine talent, were never more fully displayed. Thus directed, Gilpin rose to the occasion superbly. When the Playwright's Theater opened its fifth season, in November, 1920, it had invested all its resources and its talents in the production of *Emperor Jones.* The little audience responded to the play with frantic applause.

The first-night party upstairs was even more cheerful than usual. Punch was drunk, and everybody was praised. The Provincetowners had made a special effort and had scored a clear success. Only one drama critic had attended, but they never had worried about critics. In their relief and triumph they did not go to bed early.

Eleanor Fitzgerald went round quite late next morning to see that the Provincetown was all right. She had nothing specific to do at that hour, but there were always things to check on. To her astonishment, she found a queue in front of the box office, extending down the block.

As soon as she could believe her eyes, she dashed inside. Upstairs, the only telephone, which was inside Christine's, was madly ringing. Christine, of course, had been up late and probably was still in bed. Fitzi tore upstairs and seized the telephone from Christine's frantic mother, who was shrieking into it in her strong Danish accent, "Teeckets? Yah! Vait! Vait!"

Fitzi tried to stem the flood, but it was impossible. She could not be upstairs and down at once. She seized a moment when the telephone fell quiet to call the sleeping Players. "Get up, get up at once! The whole world's here!"

9 DEATH OF THE PROVINCETOWN

THE SUDDEN SUCCESS of the Players was not as surprising as it had appeared on the first morning. The reputation of the Provincetown had been growing for some time. First-night parties had included increasingly distinguished guests. Charlie Chaplin, then at the height of his fame, had taken the trouble to visit rehearsals of *The Emperor Jones*. Carried away by enthusiasm, he had offered to take one of the walk-on parts. He had been regretfully refused because it was obvious that people would flock to see him, not the play. That section of the public which liked to keep abreast was already conscious of the little experimental theater in the Village. It had produced *Aria da Capo*, which had later swept the country. Only its brevity had prevented Broadway from taking up *Aria da Capo*.

Meanwhile O'Neill himself was already news to the theatergoing public. He had made one hit and had been awarded a Pulitzer Prize. Managers and critics had their eye on him. To be sure, only one dramatic critic was actually present on the opening night of *The Emperor Jones*. When, however, the news was circulated that it was an extraordinary play like nothing hitherto produced, none found it incredible. All who were interested in drama rushed downtown to see for themselves.

The actual numbers of the new arrivals were not large, but the Provincetown subscribers were nearly doubled in the next few days. This created a problem for the tiny theater with its box office and telephone on different floors. What was more, the publicity was out of all proportion to this increase. The Provincetown was brought once and for all into the public eye.

An immediate and awkward result was a complaint by the New York Sabbath Committee about the Provincetown shows on Sunday evening. The little theater had always functioned as a private club because it could evade regulations which were expensive to comply with. The pretense was a thin one. If ticket purchasers were not already members, they must register as such. Membership, however, could be limited to a single performance. Luckily for the Provincetown, the judge who heard their case was a subscriber. He dismissed the complaint.

"What shall I do," inquired the police captain dolefully, "if they play again next Sunday?"

"Do something else!" snapped the judge. The Sunday performances continued.

Meanwhile, success might have been limited, but it was decisive. Impressive reviews were followed by a series of offers to move *The Emperor Jones* uptown as soon as its three-weeks' bill was over.

The Players hesitated. Their next bill was already announced. Should they allow Broadway to provide a fresh cast, or should they grab their chance to play in a real theater? If they moved uptown, they would disperse their energies, deprive their succeeding bills of some of their actors, and lose their independence. On the other hand, money and reputations would be made. Even Gilpin, who had given up his job to take the role, was getting only fifty dollars a week. Most of the rest were still unpaid, though they might have worked with the Provincetown for years. The stage designers and managers, too, would reap great benefits.

Jig protested, but he was overruled. The temptations of opportunity and fame were too great. The whole cast of *Jones* moved uptown. Jig retired in disgust to Provincetown for a while, leaving O'Neill to exploit his success. With an eye on Broadway, the Players imported a professional director to produce O'Neill's *Diff'rent*. This was another long-short play, a return to the manner of *Beyond the Horizon*.

Diff'rent soon joined *The Emperor Jones* uptown, taking its cast with it also.

Jig mourned over his theater. The Provincetown had been founded to combat the professional theater, to which it had now surrendered. He foresaw the end of his experiment, and he was right. No future performance would fail to have its eye on making money. But what he resented most of all was the attitude of O'Neill. Eugene was not above Broadway, fame, huge audiences, and money. To do him justice, he had never pretended to be so. His insistence on Broadway meeting his terms had linked him with the Provincetown, but he had always aimed at success in the professional theater. Jig talked so much and Eugene talked so little that a misunderstanding had grown up between them. Time was proving that they did not agree as well as Jig had always imagined.

It was now becoming obvious that there was a difference between the two regarding the very essence of the Provincetown's being. The little theater had become dependent on its chief dramatist. Critics, the playwright, even the cast were beginning to treat it as though it were one man's private theater. Jig Cook, who had dreamed a great dream about American drama, was not content to see his company filched from him by one artist. What of Susan Glaspell, who was his wife? What of other writers, discovered or even undiscovered yet? The Provincetown could not fulfill itself through a single talent. Yet the bigger O'Neill became, the more he demanded that the Provincetown serve his particular needs.

As the young dramatist whom he had developed leaped

into fame, Cook found himself illogically jealous. He had devoted the best years of the Provincetown to encouraging O'Neill. He had thrown himself wholeheartedly into *The Emperor Jones*. Now that O'Neill had succeeded, Jig was finding that it is hard for a man of ideas to fulfill himself by putting across those of another. Brought up to be a genius and possessed of showy talents, he had devoted his life to expressing what was in him. Why should Eugene become famous while he did not?

For all his charm and his exciting ideas, Cook had more than his share of human vanity. His discontent at this time was given emphasis by the fact that he himself had a play ready for production. *The Spring* is a play of ideas, though Cook lacked the insight to work these out in terms of human problems. One might say it was suitable for production by the Provincetown. But when it was not received with acclaim, Jig jumped too rapidly to the conclusion that the fault was in the production. He blamed the scattering of the Provincetown energies. With two plays running uptown, the Players had lost interest in anything new. Jig's father had died a little while before, and he had recently come into possession of some money. He spent a good deal of this on financing a Broadway opening for *The Spring*, which, on the third night, had four in the audience. To Jig's disagreement with the Provincetown's policies, there was now added a personal grievance against the theatrical world.

Jig Cook grew angry with O'Neill, who responded with cold indignation. No doubt Eugene despised *The Spring* and the vanity which had impelled Cook to squander his money upon it. All the old objections to Jig as director of the Provincetown became even more forcible if professional standards of acting and production were to be met. To be sure, Eugene personally owed a great deal to Jig; but in the heat of argument, the past seemed less important than the future. Each thought of the other as selfishly desiring to use the Provincetown to his own advantage.

The 1920–21 season limped to its end. Famous though it now was, the Provincetown had not succeeded with anybody but O'Neill. For the following season a play of Susan Glaspell's was actually scheduled to be moved uptown before it opened. Unluckily *The Verge*, though an interesting psychological play, was not a popular success. Its early failure was underlined by O'Neill's *Anna Christie*, which opened on Broadway in the fall of 1921, ran for nearly two hundred performances, and earned its author his second Pulitzer Prize.

It was actually difficult to fill out the Provincetown's bills. It had become too obvious that their only drawing card was O'Neill. Luckily, he still had need of an experimental theater. He had not yet reached the point where every fresh work was a theatrical event. Nor was he consistently giving of his best. He was moving away from the simplicity of *Thirst* or *Fog*, where elemental force contrasts with the insignificance of man. He was beginning to concern himself with the meaning behind the tremendous urges which dominate people. He was speculating, in fact, about life and religion. A man of emotion rather than an analytic thinker, O'Neill was struggling with

153

conceptions which constantly eluded him. In an effort to work out his philosophy through drama, he was endlessly experimenting with form and subject matter. *The Emperor Jones* had been an emotional play. In reaching for intellectual answers, O'Neill was to fail often, sometimes interestingly, but sometimes dully. He was to make theatrical history and yet in the end abandon his quest.

At this stage in O'Neill's development, both his bad works and some of his radical experiments were unattractive to Broadway managers. There was no saying whether the public would buy them. *The Straw*, his play about tuberculosis, opened in New London, where even the connection of the O'Neills with the place could not make it successful. It moved to New York in November, 1921, and closed after twenty performances.

Early in 1922, O'Neill offered *The Hairy Ape* to the Provincetown. Like *The Emperor Jones*, it was an experimental play, shorter than the traditional length. This time, however, O'Neill did not propose to entrust it to the man who had put across *The Emperor Jones*. Relations between Eugene and Cook were still deteriorating. O'Neill insisted on a professional to help with the staging and an actor he had chosen himself for the title role. He clearly intended the Provincetown run as a tryout for Broadway.

This public withdrawal of O'Neill's confidence offended Cook deeply. It robbed him of control of his own theater, in which the day of the amateur was obviously dying. The energies of the original Provincetowners had been consumed by the effort of carrying on several plays at once. It is notable that after *The Hairy Ape* they let out the Playhouse for a guest performance and concluded with a feeble comedy of Susan Glaspell's, unworthy of her talent.

With characteristic impulsiveness, Jig Cook had turned away. Gathering about him those of the original group that were left, he put through a motion closing the Provincetown for the following season. They would rent out the theater. They promised that they would open again, but the future was unsure. "It is time to go to Greece," Jig told Susan. He had always longed to tread with his own feet the soil of Athens and to feast his eyes on Delphi, home of Apollo. Without waiting for the opening of *The Hairy Ape* he sailed, taking with him Susan Glaspell, who had been, apart from O'Neill, the mainstay of the Players.

While *The Hairy Ape* was in rehearsal, Ella O'Neill had left for California, squired by Jamie, to liquidate some real-estate holdings of her husband's. Ella still wore black for James, but she now compromised with it by jewelry that she would once have considered too flashy. Her manner was gay. She was young-looking for her age, though she was troubled by headaches which she hoped the California climate would improve. Three weeks before the opening of *The Hairy Ape*, Eugene received a telegram from Jamie saying that his mother was desperately ill and a brain tumor was feared. In less than two weeks she died. Eugene, who was superintending rehearsals for *The First Man* at the Neighborhood Playhouse as well as for *The Hairy Ape*, was indispensable in New York. Communications from Jamie became increasingly erratic, and it was obvious that he was drinking again. Eugene, who had learned to know his mother during the last good years since her cure, spent a ghastly week anticipating the arrival of her body for burial near her husband, attended by Jamie in a drunken condition. On the very night of the opening of *The Hairy Ape*, he bundled Agnes and a friend off to the theater while he hurried to Grand Central. Here he found Jamie, too incoherent to locate his mother's coffin in the baggage car or arrange for it to be taken to a funeral parlor. Services were held in New York, in part to avoid comment from Ella's New London relations when Jamie was too drunk to attend them.

The long tragedy of Ella O'Neill's life was over. Jamie was deliberately drinking himself into the grave. Eugene, though distracted by sorrow, felt a real release from a past which he had hated. His desire to write about his family was no longer at war with his conscience, and as an artist he rejoiced in freedom from trammels.

Eugene's future now looked prosperous. *The Hairy Ape*, though only faintly praised by the reviewers, was making a sensation. On its first night, Macdougal Street had been blocked by long limousines. Top hats and evening dresses crowded the little ramp, and all the critics were present in a phalanx. Nor were their expectations disappointed. The sensational theme of the play for such an audience, the symbolism, use of masks—advanced techniques for their day—marked *The Hairy Ape* for success. O'Neill was already famous, though in his early thirties and with a great creative time ahead. He was even becoming rich. On the death of Jamie, their father's money, which was not inconsiderable, would be in his hands. Royalties mounted in New York. His plays were published now and commanded a large sale. European theaters were putting on performances. Eugene's reputation as the outstanding American playwright was assured.

He ought, one might suppose, to have felt confident. Artistically, he did. Personally, his private life was as much of a problem as it had always been. He had for one thing little sense about money. He never seemed to know that he could have too much of a thing that he wanted. When, later in life, his third wife introduced him to the pleasures of hand-made shoes, he acquired seventy-five pairs. All his friends noticed his absurd extravagances, which they attributed to his having been for a long time short of money. As a result, he was constantly in financial straits and resented the anxieties of this condition.

Meanwhile, his family was causing him trouble. Shane, an attractive, golden-haired little boy, was now old enough to be underfoot. Eugene was fond of him, but the fact was, he had no time for a child. All the distractions which beset the fathers of growing families were fiercely resented as interruptions of his creative work. Kathleen Jenkins, remarried but not well-to-do, had appealed to him to pay for young Eugene's education. Eugene had met the boy and liked him. It was obvious that his talents needed a better chance than Kathleen could give them. There was also Agnes's daughter Barbara, who now came occasionally to stay with her mother. All these children were irritants which might have been bearable by themselves. What made them intolerable was Eugene's relation to Agnes.

The difficulty with Agnes was that she did not consider a famous playwright as a special sort of human being. She thought it just as important that she should live her kind of life as that he should live his. He wanted seclusion. She liked society. Blossoming out with the help of more money, Agnes was making friends of her own. They were pleasant people of a rather ordinary kind, much in awe of the playwright, who felt like an animal in a zoo. He loathed being stared at, and stupid chatter was hard to bear.

From Eugene's point of view, the worst of the matter was that he needed Agnes's whole attention. He was one of those writers whose work is a terrible emotional drain. Agnes could not or would not sacrifice herself to help out. Conflicts began to flare up between them. O'Neill went through periods when he loved Agnes fiercely; he went through shattering arguments, through black resentment, hate, and love again. He disappeared in New York to drown his sorrows, or he did so at home and made violent scenes. In fact, he hardly knew how he felt about Agnes. He was only certain that she would not give him what he must have. The situation was affecting his work.

In this fashion, almost a year passed. Plans must be made about the Provincetown. Should it reopen or not? Jig Cook was still in Greece.

The Players wrote to ask for Jig's opinion, and he gave his vote against reopening. In his own terms, he was perfectly right. His dream community, his Playwright's Theater, which had introduced nearly eighty new plays by serious artists, was dead. It had been founded because Broadway was not receptive to new talent. Conditions had changed, and the Provincetown had changed them. The success of O'Neill had made a place for modern drama in the American theatrical world. New playwrights would not be slow to take advantage of this.

In this larger sense, then, Jig was right. But he had lost interest in his theater less because of its success than because of its failure. Time and events had scattered his brotherhood of artists. Of the original twenty-nine who had formed the Provincetown group, only seven had remained to sign the announcement suspending it for a year. Newer arrivals had taken the vacant places, but by no means all understood the shining ideals which Jig had shared with the postman, the milkman, the building inspector. Democracy, it seemed, worked only as long as Jig had been the chosen leader. Eventually energies had been consumed in argument, and aims had been uncertain. Jig did not want to come back, only to find his position undermined and his future as a dramatist nonexistent. He had put his heart into *The Spring* and been a failure. He had no intention at the present time of returning from Greece.

George Cook was a man who lived by enthusiasm. An extraordinary mixture of ancient glory and the simple modern life now fascinated him. Living in primitive conditions among Greek shepherds, observing the old traditions of the countryside which reached back indefinitely, he managed to arouse in his peasant neighbors a sense of their own worth and of their great heritage. Critics said scornfully that he was merely looking for easy success in surroundings less competitive than New York. In effect, however, he was displaying his remarkable talents for leadership among a primitive people who hardly knew those ancient times whose memory inspired him. The peasants of Delphi felt their lives transformed by the presence of Jig, and the Greek government took notice of the stranger in their midst as a true lover of Hellas. Absorbed in his new life, he had had enough of the Provincetown. He wished it dead.

O'Neill, on the other hand, was by no means indifferent to the fate of a theater which had always presented what he gave it. He was conscious of how much he had learned from being able to have his minor works performed. And he was still learning. Moreover, his latest plays were not among his best. *Welded*, an analysis of his relationship to Agnes, was devastatingly dismissed by a critic friend as "third-rate Strindberg." It had not yet found a producer. *The Fountain*, concerned with a quest for some ultimate value, is encumbered by a historical plot and shallow melodrama. Meanwhile, O'Neill had added to his financial embarrassments by buying a house outside New York, from which he could oversee productions without exposing himself to the hectic life of the Village. Characteristically, he had bought far more than he needed or was quite comfortable in. Brook Farm was a huge place in Ridgefield, Connecticut, complete with acres of shaven lawn, thirty-foot living room, paneled library, and servants' quarters. Its cost and upkeep increased his anxiety to get his plays before the public. Of their merits, he was convinced. It was characteristic of him that his latest creation was always something special. Only in retrospect did he regain perspective.

Thus driven by anxiety, ambition, and creative urge, O'Neill still hankered after the good days of the Province-town. It was clear to him, however, that Jig's ideal theater would no longer serve his turn. It had risen magnificently to the challenge of *The Emperor Jones*, but that had been an inspiration, a flash in the pan. O'Neill's experiments with staging were soaring beyond the resources of ama-teurs. Besides, what he ultimately needed was to get his plays before a public which was used to the professional smoothness of Broadway. In other words, O'Neill's neces-sities inspired him to look for a producer's experimental theater, not a playwright's.

He made it clear that a revival of the Provincetown must be entirely different from the past. Fresh blood was needed, along with a new view. He would not tolerate the old democratic days when everybody, theoretically at least, was as good as Jig. A production theater must be auto-cratically governed. His choice for director was Kenneth Macgowan, a friend and drama critic with practical experi-ence in the theater. Macgowan, however, associated with him Robert Edmond Jones and O'Neill himself. To mark the change, the old organization was officially dissolved. The Playwright's Theater was rechristened by its popular name of The Provincetown Playhouse. Many of the old faces were now no longer seen. The Playhouse opened in January, 1924, with *The Spook Sonata* by Strindberg, an experimental play, but neither American nor recent. The selection proclaimed that the old Provincetown was dead.

By now Jig Cook was dead, too. Cook's life had not been like that of other people, and it was appropriate that he should die in a peculiar fashion, sacrificing his life for a dog. He had a way with animals which was not shared by his Greek peasant neighbors. He had adopted a poor, ill-treated mongrel, who spent with him some months of happy life. Eventually, however, the dog fell sick and died, despite much nursing. No one diagnosed the disease; but it was glanders, a cattle ailment which is not often communicated to dogs, and very rarely to men. Jig, however, caught it. It was not easy in those remote parts to get a doctor, and his unusual illness was not diagnosed early enough to save him. Plans were made to rush him through the mountains to a hospital in Athens, but they had to be given up because it was too late. Jig died, and the whole community mourned at his funeral. Twenty years later, the peasants of Delphi were still talking about him. The Greek government gave a stone from the temple of Delphi to mark his grave.

It was a strange life and a stranger ending. What could have happened to Jig, had he lived, it is hard to say. He was getting into one of his exalted states and talking wildly about entering a Greek Orthodox monastery. Poor Susan was finding him difficult indeed, and yet she never felt that his possibilities had been exhausted. Who knows what he might have achieved? The Provincetown is a richer monument to him than a stone from Delphi.

For the opening of *Spook Sonata*, the new Provincetown had been painted, the stage enlarged, the seats numbered. It boasted a press agent, and its first nights were formal occasions. Despite these improvements, *Spook Sonata* was not a success It was followed by *Fashion* a revival of a little Victorian comedy beautifully staged by Robert Edmond Jones. This was a real hit. The Provincetown took over the Greenwich Village Theater for the rest of its run, in order to free the Provincetown stage for *All God's Chillun* and a Molière which had been put on while the O'Neill was in rehearsal.

A great uproar now began when it was realized that the Provincetown had engaged a Negro actor, young Paul Robeson, to play the husband of a white woman. Curiously enough, O'Neill had hardly conceived *All God's Chillun* as an analysis of social conditions. Its black hero, Jim, and its white heroine, Ella, are his parents, whose ill-assorted marriage he is probing. The color problem is merely a way of concealing his personal involvement. The last of the unhappy O'Neills, Eugene felt free to write about his family, though for the present he distorted the circumstances of their lives.

The papers, seizing on a sensation with glee, now pointed out that at one point in the play, which had already been published, the white girl kisses her Negro husband's hand. The Provincetown's actors were harassed by anonymous letters, threats from the Ku Klux Klan, a bomb warning, and other such crude and mindless gestures. The mayor was appealed to on the grounds that the play would incite a riot. Accordingly, on the late afternoon of opening day, the mayor's office refused to license the child-actors who appeared in the first scene. Police were stationed through the theater to be sure the edict was obeyed.

The natural result was to give *All God's Chillun* a great deal of free publicity. When the play opened in May,

1924, James Light came before the curtain to explain the mayor's action and offer to read the children's scene. From that moment, the popularity of the play was assured. The critics did not think highly of it, and with fair justice. However, the public appetite for sensation sustained it till the end of the Provincetown's season, when it transferred to the Greenwich Village and played through the summer.

Success of this sort enlarged the opportunities of the new directors of the Provincetown. *Fashion* had really made money, and they decided to take the Greenwich Village Theater as well. The more professional their productions became, the more they depended on earnings. Jig's total outlay for *The Emperor Jones* had been five hundred and two dollars. He had beggared the treasury for his dome and almost faced a revolution. The production of *Fashion* alone had cost ten times as much. This was a sum which could not be recouped from the tiny audiences of the Provincetown. The Greenwich Village, with a larger capacity, was better suited to present needs. Accordingly, the three directors announced that the Provincetown was to remain experimental, while the Greenwich Village was to play repertory. Actually both were O'Neill theaters and produced in the single season of 1924–25 the *S.S. Glencairn* plays, a revival of *Diff'rent*, a short play called *The Triumph of the Egg*, and *Desire Under the Elms*, an undoubted masterpiece.

The production of all these plays, with the addition of Gilbert and Sullivan's *Patience*, Congreve's *Love for Love*, and a couple of experimental plays at the Provincetown proved a fearful strain on the united staff. Storage of expensive scenery was becoming a great problem. Neither place had room for the sets, while city regulations about warehousing and fire precautions raised the cost of keeping them elsewhere. Other difficulties multiplied. A subscription audience for two theaters together was hard to gather. Backers, so necessary now, were unenthusiastic about the joint enterprise. Lack of office space prevented coordination of activity. Properties, programs, costumes, or messages were daily rushed back and forth between the theaters. Perpetual emergencies, openings, closings, meetings, rehearsals made up a dizzying round for people attempting to be in both theaters at once.

At first the Provincetown had made a conscious effort to keep up the spirit of the old days. Christine had moved away when the group was suspended, but weekly dinners together were arranged. Without Jig Cook, there were few of the old discussions about creative activity. Everybody talked shop. People argued about lighting, sets, publicity, details of acting. They discussed promotion plans. Actors talked over the techniques of voice production or their lessons in eurythmics.

It did not take very long for a rift to develop. It was clear that the present confusion could not go on. The Provincetown, too small to make real money, was soon regarded as a liability. Even the Greenwich Village was a problem in this respect. *Desire Under the Elms*, though not highly praised by critics, was enjoying a successful run. Yet money came in too slowly to suit O'Neill, who had decided to get away from Brook Farm by wintering in Bermuda. When he found the complications of his life too great, he tended to seek a solution by establishing himself elsewhere, regardless of expense. His menagerie of children was about to be increased. Agnes was pregnant, and Eugene was visibly nervous at the prospect of another baby in the house. It had not occurred to him as yet to try the expedient of running away from Agnes altogether.

Money became available soon. The theme of *Desire Under the Elms*, involving incest, was controversial. Abbie Putnam has married Ephraim Cabot to get a home and is determined to possess his farm after his death. Equally insistent is Eben, Ephraim's grown son, who regards the inheritance as his right. Abbie persuades the doting Ephraim to leave the farm to her child if she shall have one. Then she casts her eye on Eben to provide the boy which Ephraim is too old to give her. At this moment calculation breaks down. The young man and the young woman are drawn to each other with a force which neither can withstand. When the child is born and the truth comes out, the angry Ephraim disillusions his son about Abbie. But she by now is ready to prove by desperate means that she truly loves Eben. If the child-heir is to come between them, she will kill it. She does and Eben, appalled but convinced, takes his stand by her to claim a share in her guilt. They are arrested together.

This powerful and beautifully constructed play moved uptown, where it attracted the attention of a district attorney who was anxious to clean up Broadway. He gave the producers a few days to close it, failing which he proposed to bring the matter before a grand jury. The sensation naturally benefited *Desire*, which was exonerated by a citizen play-jury selected to go and see it. Its popularity was further assured by its being banned in Boston and having its whole cast arrested in Los Angeles.

Desire solved O'Neill's financial problems for the immediate moment, but it did not heal the split among the Provincetown Players. The leaders of the old guard now were James Light and Eleanor Fitzgerald. Both of these had joined the Provincetown before its move to 133. Neither was a creative artist. Eleanor Fitzgerald, tall, red-haired, good-looking, conservatively dressed, had been office secretary, business manager, financial expert, errand boy, and universal friend since the moment of her joining. In a difficulty, everybody confided in Fitzi. It was she who got things done. Everything was her job, from raising money to getting the programs printed or finding cleaners. Fitzi was the expert who could run business affairs with the minimum equipment and occasional voluntary aid in addressing envelopes. Fitzi really loved the Provincetown. She found her work fun. But she had in her own way as great a need of self-expression as Jig Cook did in his. Fitzi needed a cause. She had joined the Provincetown at the end of World War I after devoting herself for nearly two years to a fight for amnesty for political prisoners. Now, after feeding on the high-souled aspirations of Jig, it was not in her nature to come down to earth with Macgowan or to care for the practical business of launching O'Neill's plays on uptown runs.

James Light, who had given up his career to the Provincetown, was also one of those without whom the little theater would have been unthinkable. He had been in turn actor, stage manager, producer, had gained a reputation in the professional theater, and had been entrusted with larger production jobs. The Provincetown, however, was his real home. Both he and Eleanor Fitzgerald were directly affected by the hectic confusion of running two theaters at once. And both, though really professional, were used to amateur economies for which the new directors, if successful, had no need. There was really some question whether either of them would find a place in the Provincetown's future.

There were still other semi-amateurs who felt the same way. Their eyes were not on Broadway. They wanted to get back to the good old days when productions were within a low financial range and plays were truly experimental. Why should they change their nature merely because they had nursed a playwright who had succeeded?

Everybody's interests pointed in the same direction. Macgowan and O'Neill were glad to be rid of the Provincetown, which never paid. Fitzgerald and Light were anxious to take it over, relying on a revival of the good old spirit and backed by the new reputation. On this basis, the separation was arranged. The Provincetown had brought out its last new O'Neill. Though Eugene remained nominally on the board, he had grown beyond them. *The Great God Brown*, on which he had then been working, was out of their range. *Lazarus Laughed*, which was to follow, beggared the resources even of the professional stage. His mammoth dramas, ushered in by *Strange Interlude*, were far beyond the capabilities of the Players. If Light and Fitzgerald were to make a creative thing out of the new Provincetown, they must look elsewhere for fresh talent.

Meanwhile, O'Neill's new dramas went to the triumvirate at the Greenwich Village. Actually this was a poor bargain for them, though the fact was not yet apparent. In 1926, *The Fountain* and *The Great God Brown* were ambitious failures. Presently O'Neill was to soar beyond the Greenwich Village. In fact, he was heading for a complete break with his old life. Success had only added, as far as he could see, to his personal problems. His escape outlet, as usual, had been drink. Eventually, however, he was coming to perceive that months of abstinence punctuated by week-long orgies would not do. He was not getting younger and had always been nervous about his health. He began to feel he would have to choose between this weakness and his work. Once the matter presented itself to him in this fashion, the outcome of a long inner battle was inevitable. His creative impulse was by far the strongest thing in his life. It had already saved him, as nothing else could have done, from becoming a hopeless alcoholic like his brother. With the aid of some psychiatric help, he now at last gave up liquor. The result was, he had no refuge left. The old release from tension, sorrow, despair, or fury was no longer available to him. He needed the abnormal devotion which he vainly demanded from Agnes more than ever.

O'Neill had taken his troubles to Bermuda and now seldom came to New York. When he did so, he was little concerned with the new Provincetown, which had started out with high hopes, recovering some of the old Players and including Jig Cook's daughter Nilla in a walk-on part. But the whole atmosphere of Greenwich Village had changed since World War I. It had become almost fashionable. Rents had gone up. Young people either could not or would not live on a few dollars a week. Solid dinners like Polly's or Christine's were not available for around fifty cents. The cheapest place for artists and writers in the postwar world was no longer Greenwich Village, but Paris, where whole blocks were now English-speaking. The new Provincetown commanded neither the talent nor the devotion it had done in the early days.

In a changed world, the little theater was living on its past. Respectable elderly ladies were invading its audience now. Jig's stirring sayings were chiefly useful to help Fitzi raise the money which she got together by constant miracles of effort and devotion. The past contained the second Provincetown, too, the professional era. Without losing precious patronage, it was never possible for Fitzi and Light to break away from that. Thirteen-dollar productions, alas, were gone for ever.

Light was not the man Jig Cook had been. As general manager, he was no doubt far more competent. But his judgment was not always sound, and his personality lacked Jig's compelling force. He made favorites, offered large parts to new people, or consoled malcontents with a raise in salary out of proportion to that of others.

Nothing went smoothly. The little theater was growing dilapidated, and there was no money for repairs. Even a hit hardly put the Provincetown in funds. Two hundred and twenty seats no longer carried its expenses.

A new production involved fresh outlay. Plays were kept running long after interest had died because no capital was available for anything new, while almost any income was better than an empty theater. For the same reason, a new play could not be planned or in rehearsal while the old one lingered on. Only when it utterly died would the management scurry around and then eventually put on another, too often indifferent production.

Had this been all, the Provincetown would have lasted hardly a season. Now and then, however, productions scored a success. In desperate moments, they could revive O'Neill. On other occasions, they followed Macgowan's example with popular revivals of older plays. But experimentation was part of their policy, too. Lacking the inspiration of Jig, they were in no position to encourage dramatists by staging indifferent plays. The days when a single good one-acter could carry a bill of three were over now. In choosing full-length drama, discretion was needed.

Such a situation could not continue indefinitely. But institutions like the Provincetown which have had vitality retain a great capacity for survival. Among those interested in the little theater, Otto Kahn now took the lead. If the Provincetown were to be established on a more permanent basis, the Players, he pointed out, must abandon their theater. The smallness and discomfort of the Playhouse were great liabilities. For a New York, as opposed to a Village audience, Macdougal Street was inaccessible. Its single advantage, in fact, was cheapness of operation. What the Players needed was a decent stage, a larger theater, and a money-raising campaign. Kahn paid two months' rent on the Garrick, and he started a campaign for five thousand ten-dollar subscriptions, plus a seventy-thousand-dollar production fund.

The period was the end of the booming twenties when everybody felt rich and generous. Response was wholehearted.

The move took place at once, and an enlarged board was created to share the load with James Light and Eleanor Fitzgerald. It was a typical businessman's board whose members, established in other fields, were devoting a couple of hours in the week to the Provincetown. It was elderly and far from unanimous. Some were terrified at the risks they were all taking. Others were in an expansive mood. In the selection of plays, an immediate decision, their instinct was to play safe. Two plays, both mediocre, were put in production while the new situation settled down. But time had run out for the Provincetown at last. The great stock-market crash of 1929 interrupted its season. Fund-raising stopped, and pledges were not honored. On December 14, 1929, the Provincetown Players closed their doors.

10   THE BREAK

THE DEATH of the Provincetown was in a sense a formality, since the links between it and its past had already been broken. Indeed, Susan Glaspell, returning from Greece in deep mourning, had taken exception to the name of the Provincetown Playhouse. Macgowan's theater had abandoned the creative principles on which it had been founded and had no right to call itself the Provincetown. O'Neill was at pains to smooth her feelings, pointing out that the Playhouse was a fitting memorial and offering to have a plaque placed upon it in memory of Jig. He owed George Cook a great deal and could afford to be generous, though in the heat of controversy he had accused him of driving talent away and then deserting.

The Provincetown kept its name, but the plaque was not put up. Susan Glaspell wrote no more plays for Jig's little theater. At the moment she was concerned with a book to commemorate Jig and planning a novel on her experience in Greece. The immediate past was too poignant for her to put it aside. It was a few years before Susan's dramatic talent blossomed out into *Alison's House*, a Broadway hit and a Pulitzer Prize winner.

Even before the Provincetown closed, the Greenwich Village Theater had failed. A really good O'Neill might have prolonged its life, but in this respect, the Greenwich Village was unlucky. O'Neill was seriously disturbed by its collapse. For the first time since the reading of *Bound East for Cardiff* he was without what amounted to his private theater.

The void was soon filled. Lawrence Langner, who had founded the Washington Square Theater and thus indirectly inspired the Provincetown, had closed his operation during the war. Shortly after, he had started up again with a subscription audience which was far more ambitious than that of the Provincetown. Increasingly wealthy from his patent business, and in touch with forward-looking patrons of the theater, he found funds to do what the Provincetown could not. He built a theater and profited from the growth of interest in serious drama. The repertory of the Guild Theater was not experimental or all-American. It introduced the best of contemporary drama, interspersed with popular revivals. For many years it presented the latest Shaw to the American public.

The strength of the Guild Theater lay in its subscription audience. Season tickets assured a fair hearing, even for an indifferent play. Connections in Chicago, Boston, San Francisco, and other cities made tours possible under similar conditions. In short, Lawrence Langner had developed a successful method of making the production of serious drama a profitable business.

For such a theater, O'Neill was an obvious choice. In 1927, arrangements for the production of *Marco Millions* and *Strange Interlude* were made with the Guild. The great success of the latter confirmed O'Neill and Langner in their alliance. Henceforward, an outlet for an O'Neill play was assured.

The break between the Provincetown and the playwright whom it had made famous was complete. Even the personal links between O'Neill and the Village characters who had contributed to his rise were being severed. This is not to say he was unmindful of them all. Terry Carlin and a few other pensioners received from him a small weekly sum. But he did not see Terry any more. How could they get together without drinking? He had always shown a startling willingness to sacrifice friendships to his convenience—which meant, it is only fair to say, the demands of his work. When he and Agnes had moved into the old Coast Guard station in Peaked Hill Bars, they had owned a dilapidated shed which for several summers was the home of Terry Carlin. Here Terry made blueberry wine and attempted disastrously to get drunk on shellac. Indeed, Terry became a sort of extra male nurse to Shane, neither of whose parents had a great deal of time to supervise him. Terry had the run of the house, to the distaste of the respectable cook on whom domestic happiness depended. One day she came to O'Neill in a fine fury. The dirty old man had spat in her clean sink. Either he must stay out of the house or she would leave it. O'Neill, though no doubt with reluctance, sacrificed Terry. A well-run house was essential to his work.

Nowadays, O'Neill did not go to Provincetown, and while in New York he avoided the Village. His friends among the Provincetowners had to some extent been boon companions. None of them had drunk so much as he, but they had drunk with him. Their very presence was a temptation to indulge in an orgy. Eugene was making new friends; dramatic critics, producers, theater people in the great world of Broadway. In fact, his attachment to the Provincetowners was becoming nominal.

The big house in Ridgefield was his first attempt to avoid the temptations of the Village. It did not work. Friends came up for weekends, and O'Neill drank with them. Nor did he like the Ridgefield place once he had it. Presently he and Agnes moved down to Bermuda, where they soon decided to live for nine months of the year. Without waiting to dispose of the Ridgefield place, or even of their summer home in Provincetown, they bought a Bermuda house to which they planned great alterations.

O'Neill, it appears, was seeking various outlets for the emotional pressures which had previously driven him to drink. Unfortunately the expedient of moving from one place to the next had only a temporary effect. He liked new scenes, most particularly if they were near the sea. He enjoyed situations where he did not know anybody and could ration his contacts. He got an excitement out of planning ideal houses. Pretty soon, however, when alterations were actually begun, their inconveniences drove him wild. In Bermuda, Agnes took comfortably to the wealthy Bermuda crowd. She stood up for her rights, and she was not clever in keeping her husband and her new friends apart.

Actually the main trouble with Bermuda was that Eugene's whole relation with Agnes was growing unbearable. Her inability to measure up to his standards of devotion grated on him the more because he could not drown fury in liquor. The Bermuda house, like all homes Agnes had, was sloppily run. Someone unkindly said it had an atmosphere of lamb stew and diapers. No sooner had Shane grown old enough to demand less attention than baby Oona had arrived. Trivial upsets led to shattering quarrels. These were followed by periods of smoldering anger. The situation was uncomfortable enough to embarrass visitors.

In the summer of 1926, the O'Neills returned to New England, but not to Provincetown. Elisabeth Marbury, partner to Eugene's agent, had a summer place in Maine, near which she persuaded O'Neill to establish himself. Young Eugene, now sixteen years old, was asked up for the summer, together with Barbara Burton, Agnes's daughter, who was twelve. Shane was seven and Oona still a baby. No doubt O'Neill wanted to see something of young Eugene, to whom he had taken a great fancy ever since their first meeting, some four years back. Barbara had a right to spend an occasional time with her mother. All the same, the ill-assorted ménage drove O'Neill almost mad.

While matters were in this state, Elisabeth Marbury invited a guest to stay. Carlotta Monterey, born Hazel Tharsing, was an actress now in her late thirties. Dark, white-skinned, spectacular in appearance, she had chosen her stage name to harmonize with her Spanish looks. Her stage career had been successful rather than brilliant, partly because she had never pursued it with real ardor. More famous as a beauty than an actress, she had married three times and, coming into a large sum of money, had given up her profession. Four years before this, however, she had been induced to take the part of Mildred in the *Hairy Ape* when it left the Provincetown to move uptown. This had been done at the insistence of the director, who had not liked the girl with whom the Provincetown had opened. Carlotta had fitted well into the Provincetown group but had not cared for O'Neill, who had appeared only once and had never even thanked her for taking on the part in the midst of its run. Indeed, he evidently had not cared for her acting. She decided he was an awful man with the rudest manners. It by no means pleased her when Miss Marbury told her the O'Neills were coming to tea.

This time Eugene seemed to try to be friendly. It was Agnes to whom Carlotta took a dislike. Agnes was showing off. No one knows what her relation to Eugene was at that instant or what unease possessed her. Perhaps her behavior inspired Eugene to make some amends. At all events, when Carlotta was asked to take him down to the bathouse for a swim, he apologized for their previous meeting, explaining that he had come straight to *The Hairy Ape* from seeing his mother's body laid out for burial. The excuse, of course, won instant sympathy. Ella's burial had actually taken place a few weeks earlier while the *Ape* was at the Provincetown. O'Neill was dramatizing, though his grief for his mother may genuinely have been the cause of his abruptness.

Carlotta Monterey was a positive person capable of strong dislikes. Yet to those who pleased her, she was kindness itself. Her sympathy went out to O'Neill, and liking followed when he came out of the bathhouse clad in the only bathing suit he found there—one belonging to his hostess, who was elderly and large. O'Neill, who wanted his swim, was perfectly unself-conscious about this ridiculous costume. She liked that and admired the magnificent way in which he was at home in the water. In fact, she felt that she would enjoy seeing more of him.

Soon the two were meeting fairly often—by coincidence it appeared. When they met in company, they talked together. At the end of the summer, Agnes and her children sailed for Bermuda, while Eugene put up at the Harvard Club in New York. He really did have business in New York, but his bachelor life and his absence from his old haunts left him at loose ends. He called constantly on Carlotta, who had divorced her third husband a year before and was living alone in an apartment. This was immaculate and beautifully furnished, as every place belonging to Carlotta always was. In it they had time for real tête-à-têtes. He told her of the childhood sufferings which still haunted him. She showed him, perhaps without needing to say much, her understanding of the untroubled life he wanted to live and her great capacity for organizing smoothly.

"I need you, I need you," he told her frantically. The appeal tore at her heart, even while she noticed that he never said, "I love you." He did, however. For all his obsession with Carlotta, the tie with Agnes was not easy to break. He could not have torn free if he had not felt the greatest passion of his life.

It took him well over a year to decide what to do. He spent most of it in Bermuda, failing to live on friendly terms with Agnes and longing for Carlotta. In November, 1927, he was again in New York, attending the rehearsals of *Marco Millions* and *Strange Interlude*, both of which were due to open in January. He had made up his mind to elope with Carlotta, yet he still wrote to Agnes and asked her to come to New York. She refused. Though aware of his entanglement, she insisted on regarding it as a temporary affair. She may have felt, moreover, that face to face she was no match for a famous beauty, immaculately groomed and independently wealthy. She refused to talk about divorce and stayed in Bermuda.

Quietly O'Neill and Carlotta left for Europe early in 1928. Nothing was settled. O'Neill gave the Provincetown house to Eugene Junior. The Ridgefield house and his parents' New London estate were still unsold. Eugene wrote to eight-year-old Shane, "Always remember that I love you and Oona an awful lot." Carlotta, more frank about her feelings, left her own Cynthia, who was eleven years old, with her mother. Truth was, the two desired life together without interference.

The sensational elopement of America's foremost playwright coincided with the smashing success of *Strange Interlude*. The popularity of this play proved greater than that of anything O'Neill had written yet, and it earned him more than a quarter of a million dollars and a third Pulitzer Prize. For his private life, the timing was unfortunate. He and Carlotta were forced to desperate expedients to protect themselves from reporters. On one occasion he shipped under a false name, disguised as a minister—to no avail. Motoring in Southern France and Spain, he had a friend send him picture postcards from Germany which he filled out and sent back there to have mailed to America, thus misleading his closest connections about where he was. The situation grated on his nerves until he turned in fury on the cause of all his misery—the unfairness of Agnes.

Faced by the fact that her husband had finally left her, Agnes at first held out against divorce. Perhaps she still thought he might repent of what he had done. At all events, she told the papers that her husband was on holiday in Europe, while she knew nothing of the whereabouts of Miss Monterey. Time passed, and angry letters crossed the Atlantic. Eventually lawyers were set to discuss divorce.

Eugene was beside himself with anger when he discovered that Agnes insisted on more money than he thought he should provide. It had always, he protested, been understood between them that their marriage should be dissolved if either fell out of love. Agnes was trying to get out of keeping her word. Not only was she demanding an extravagant sum for herself, but she was asking four times more for the support of Shane and Oona than he had paid for young Eugene's education.

We can hardly fail to sympathize with Agnes. Infuriating she may have been, but her position was not unreasonable. She had largely sacrificed what might have been a full-time writing career, and she had two young children, not to mention Barbara. Eugene was just turning forty, world-famous, fairly rich, and with presumably productive years ahead. He was about to make a wealthy match. The actual details of the final settlement seem modest. Eugene's indignation was forced on him by his conscience, not by Agnes. It was easier to justify what he had done if he could hate Agnes wholeheartedly. In the year and a half of delays which preceded his divorce, he learned to do just that. He went through a mental hell out of which on two occasions he escaped with alcohol, only to face a shattering quarrel with Carlotta, followed by physical and nervous collapse. When in July, 1929, he was free to marry, he had sworn revenge on Agnes if he could get it. Shane and Oona, whom he had loved "an awful lot," were merely Agnes's children now. Rather than share them with her, he preferred to neglect them.

He could not live without Carlotta. She made him the perfect wife, and he adored her. She knew how to live as he wanted to live. She persuaded him to rent a

French castle in Touraine with forty-five rooms, battlements, and family heirlooms. She put in modern plumbing and made it comfortable without electricity or central heating. She ran the servants and spoke the French, devoting her days to smoothing life for Eugene. Her use of luxury was imaginative. She taught him to like good clothes and expensive cars, to rest his eyes casually on objects of beauty. She saw to it that he was stimulated by just the right number of distinguished guests. When they dined alone, Carlotta dressed for him as formally as for a great party. Unobtrusive when he wanted to write, she was always ready to fit into his hours of relaxation. If he desired to tell her what he was doing, she had been an actress and understood his work in technical terms.

Early in their life together, Eugene had asked Carlotta to take over correspondence and telephone calls. From this point onward, few got a letter from Eugene unless it was on important theatrical business. Nor did Carlotta hesitate to weed out his friends, particularly any who had known Agnes well or with whom Eugene used to drink.

The Provincetowners were among the first to be cast off. Mary Vorse and Susan Glaspell wrote their good wishes to him on his marriage. They were fond of Agnes, but they wished Eugene happiness and thought it none of their business to take sides. They were never answered. Later they heard through the grapevine that Eugene had complained he was hurt because they had not written. They knew who sorted the mail. Yet Carlotta's action, if she did indeed take it, was in general accord with Eugene's own views. He really wanted her to keep crowds away and simplify his living. He seldom made intimate friends. Many people with whom he had once been familiar meant little to him when the reason for their acquaintanceship was over. Besides, he was retreating from novelty and experiment. His mink-lined overcoat, his chauffeur, his Renault had nothing to do with his past bohemian life. Carlotta was a complete contrast both to Agnes and to his drug-sodden mother, unable even to provide the family meals.

He was being isolated by Carlotta's loving care from the past which represented so much misery to his mind. Even friends who got answers from Carlotta often gave up the effort of corresponding with a woman whom they personally hardly knew. She might, for one thing, never show their letters to Eugene. She was not eager for intimacy with people who had nothing to contribute to Eugene's career. He was becoming an object of pilgrimage to theatrical people in New York. They went to him by invitation, which was hard to get. But once invited, they were royally entertained.

Agnes herself may have been happier without Eugene. They were not well mated. His moods, his drinking, his occasional violence cannot have made him easy to live with. Agnes fell in love again and, eventually, married. All three children suffered from a neglect which paralleled too closely that of Eugene's childhood. Both boys were sent to boarding school even earlier than their father. Both suffered greatly. Both had inherited their fair share of the difficult temperament of the O'Neills. Little Oona was too young to remember her father. Only young Eugene, who was grown, had any contact with the playwright through the years which immediately followed. The break was complete.

11   CARLOTTA'S YEARS

THE NEW LIFE of Eugene O'Neill brought relief from
pressure and bliss such as he had never known. To those
friends to whom he still wrote, he could hardly find words
to express his happiness. Carlotta and he were together.
Intrusive reporters or quarrels with Agnes could not disturb
their inner life. Yet even while Eugene wrote in these
terms, he was being driven almost distracted by the publicity of his affair and the demands of Agnes.

In the midst of these alternations between bitterness

and joy, he produced *Dynamo*, a poor play crammed with spite. Later on, O'Neill dismissed it with a shrug. He ought never to have written while he was so tormented by Agnes's behavior. This may be so, yet the play holds interest. The creative impulse of O'Neill was firmly rooted in misery and anger, not in joy. His new happiness had no effect on it. What would happen when Carlotta with painstaking care removed all sources of friction? What would nourish the playwright in his ivory tower to which the thundering echoes of Hitler's advance across Europe came as a faint mutter? What would he find to resent in the midst of luxury? What frustration could he encounter in success?

To those who asked such questions, Eugene seemed to give an answer with what he himself called "Carlotta's play." *Mourning Becomes Electra* is his most ambitious effort and to many his greatest. In length it compares to *Strange Interlude* and in dramatic tension to *Desire Under the Elms*. But in *Strange Interlude* the personality of Nina hardly justifies the scale of O'Neill's study. His true heroine is the Life-Force, whose abstract power is not always real enough to lift individual scenes. In *Mourning Becomes Electra*, the characters of Lavinia and her mother are on a great scale. If something dark and cosmic looms behind them, they feel themselves a part of it and do not prattle unmeaningly, as Nina often does. Thus the lurid or melodramatic becomes moving because they make it so. The huge play forms one whole. Its force is concentrated. Indeed, its power is the most obvious thing about it.

Mourning Becomes Electra is therefore Carlotta's vindication. She had made herself nurse, companion, housekeeper, secretary, and friend, even mother to O'Neill as well as wife. She had set him free from material worries as far as it was possible to do so. He had responded by a tremendous play. If he was capable of this vast effort now, what might not follow?

It is an interesting question. Carlotta had given O'Neill leisure to concentrate his creative powers. But as a result, *Mourning Becomes Electra* is a developed, rather than an experimental play. O'Neill is no longer pressing forward to capture the inexpressible. The resources of the stage are not insufficient for him now. He is using what he has learned, not reaching for more. Nor is he dashing off his lines with the same excitement as in the past. *Mourning Becomes Electra* took nearly two years to complete. It bears marks of thought and study which had never before appeared in O'Neill to such a degree. Hitherto his impact had been emotional.

Even more notable is the fact that O'Neill is turning more than ever to his past for the impulses which bring forth tragedy. For all its pretensions to elemental grandeur, his play is an analysis of family life. Its incidents and characters bear small relation to the O'Neills, but its emotions are perceptibly Eugene's own. Would his stored-up miseries be great enough to carry him through Carlotta's stormless world where discontents must come from within?

In 1931, the O'Neills returned to New York to attend the rehearsals of *Mourning Becomes Electra*, which was to open at the Guild Theater that fall. They came as celebrities, and sensation attended their coming. Ralph Barton, who had been Carlotta's previous husband, celebrated the occasion by shooting himself through the head. He had long been a victim of mental depression, and in the separation he had been at fault. He did not deny these facts, but he left a letter in which he regretted the loss of his angel Carlotta, "the one person who could have saved me." Too late he added, "She did her best." The reporters, of course, were out in platoons, while Barton's brother was willing to state that the loss of Carlotta had broken Ralph's heart. White and shaking, O'Neill answered what questions he must and dodged the others, once leaving the theater over the roof of a skating rink next door. Eventually sensation died down, but the incident confirmed him in his determination to get out of New York.

His old life, it was evident, was as dead as the Provincetown. The little house in Peaked Hill Bars which James had given to his son and Agnes had fallen victim to the encroaching seas. Young Eugene, who had distinguished himself at Yale, was about to get married. Shane and Oona, shy and silent with their father, came to be introduced. To share anything with Agnes was impossible for Eugene. He let his rights over the children go by default and shelved the problem.

Carlotta indulged him as always. The lease on their château had still a year to run. It did not matter. The great depression held the western world in its grip, but the O'Neills hardly reduced expenditures. Eugene had his Cadillac, bought almost new from some bankrupt tycoon, and his chauffeur because he did not like to drive in traffic. Presently they fixed on Sea Island, off the Georgia coast, as being remote enough from the hustle of Broadway or the inquisitiveness of the papers. They built their own hundred-thousand-dollar house, a vast expenditure in days when materials and labor were going cheap. Eugene had his study furnished like a ship and with curved windows looking out to sea. Carlotta had her formal garden and vast living room. There was a sandy beach behind. An eight-foot wall surrounded the whole to insure privacy.

Here Eugene could work and swim all winter long. Isolated by his island and his wall as securely as he had been in France by his lack of mastery of the language, he saw nobody except by invitation. Once more everything that could please him was provided, often before he could realize a need. To be sure, the climate was not quite perfect. Summer was oppressively hot and humid. There were rattlesnakes and coral snakes. Carlotta had to have the bushes clipped a foot above the ground. O'Neill was at work on a play based on his marriage to Carlotta which was no better than *Dynamo*, based on his marriage to Agnes. *Days Without End* is not venomous, but conveys a feeling of futility. What is life about? The hero, John Loving, has left and finally returns to the Catholic Church. Yet his wrestling with his wife's soul and his own seems singularly barren. The quest of *Lazarus Laughed* and *The Great God Brown* is being re-enacted in a more obvious form. In the earlier plays we can at least believe that O'Neill's searching might find some ultimate creed. Now we are less sure.

It was not for lack of effort that O'Neill failed. He battered his brains and his emotions as relentlessly for *Days Without End* as he had done for *Mourning Becomes Electra*. Indeed, the work was more taxing just because the central problem which obsessed his mind was not being solved. He gave the script to Carlotta inscribed in his own hand, "This, Our Pangs Without End."

Frustrating as this was, it had one fruitful issue. In reaction his brain turned, unprompted, away. In September, 1932, he woke up one morning with the scenario of a complete play in his mind. By that afternoon it was already on paper. Six weeks later his only comedy, *Ah, Wilderness!*, was finished.

It was a true aberration from O'Neill's style. He was not without humor, but he saw life in stark terms. Existence was nothing to smile at, except perhaps in dreams. Yet at this time, if at any, he was happy. The frenzy and bliss of his first year with Carlotta were behind him. Life was tranquil now. He possessed everything he wanted. He had no encumbering ties. "Why not," some voice must have said, "take life easy? Why eternally struggle with the world, the past, oneself? Is it not possible to look on and to smile?" For six weeks he did so and, refreshed, plunged back into "Pangs Without End."

Poor Carlotta! Pride herself she might when the genius was fruitful, yet she must also have longed to make him happy. He adored her, was dependent on her loving care every hour of the day. He had no friends apart from her, no pleasures, almost no opinions or thoughts, save those of that tormented self which she could never share. How could she build up his peace of mind without starving his great creative powers? The delicate question may have vexed her often. But inscrutable Fate smiled at her efforts. It had its own miseries in store, soon to be felt.

Life ran in a regular groove by now. Sea Island began to pall like every other retreat. They moved to Seattle, then on to San Francisco. Thirty miles outside the latter they built themselves a "pseudo-Chinese" house on the side of a mountain facing a breath-taking view. O'Neill had a swimming pool from which the panorama spread out in its immensity. Carlotta battled with the servant problem and defended his privacy tooth and nail. It was becoming hard work.

In 1936, O'Neill had been awarded the Nobel Prize for Literature. Though naturally flattered by the congratulations pouring in, he could not face the trip to Sweden, speech, and ceremony. Luckily, as it must have appeared to him then, his health was giving him trouble. He was really ill, as it turned out. Appendicitis, neuritis, kidney trouble, and an uncontrollable tremor all beset him. Not yet fifty, he now looked older. His attitudes of mind were hardening, too.

Mourning Becomes Electra had reached a high crest of success, but ambition to prove himself still greater had swept him onward. He had taken up a mammoth project calculated to make even *Electra* look small. It was to consist of a whole cycle, delving deeply into the influences, personal and social, which had dominated his family. Put briefly, it was the history of an Irish immigrant family which, joining in the American struggle for wealth and power, lost its own soul. It was to become his last word on his past, a tremendous denunciation of that material prosperity which he envied, grabbed greedily when it came, and loathed in others. He found the new concept intensely hard work, but it possessed him. At times he would write through the night, while real people receded from his world. His definition of a friend was gradually becoming one who made few demands. Meanwhile, melancholia deepened as his health declined. Carlotta's problems were increasing unmanageably. Servants were becoming hard to get. Her way of living was outmoded, yet she needed to give her playwright more attendance, and not less.

Ten weeks in hospital and two operations at the beginning of 1937 improved matters, and yet Eugene never entirely recovered. He plunged back into work which went on slowly because of neuritis, black depression, and the increasing tremor of his hands. Nor could he isolate himself from the news. It was soon impossible to ignore the events leading up to World War II. In 1940, he and Carlotta agonized over the fall of France, where they had spent two happy years. Yet World War II was not a creative force in O'Neill's mind. It was rather a dreadful distraction from his work. He had spun himself a cocoon inside which he lived. New emotions and outer contacts were irrelevant to it.

Three times in the ensuing years he turned away from his cycle as he had turned before from his "Pangs Without End." But the results this time were not tender comedies. *The Iceman Cometh, A Moon for the Misbegotten,* and *A Long Day's Journey Into Night* are at once the most personal and the most hopeless of his plays. It was for the last that O'Neill was posthumously awarded a fourth Pulitzer Prize. The sensation that they convey is that of failure. In the *Iceman,* Larry, whose compassion for his fellows lightens the play, is left face to face with himself, perceiving in his mirror a dirty, frightened old man, too cowardly to live or die. Josie, heroine of the *Moon*, finds her romantic moment a sham, the object of her love a leaky balloon which never will get off the ground. A *Long Day's Journey* hardly even makes a concession to the illusion of hope. No passing gleam of sunshine lights it up. Eugene O'Neill relives his past. He finds it agonizing. He finds also that it has done no good, conveyed no meaning. In that case, how could he complete an epic cycle summing up this identical past? That he brought great gifts and strong emotions to the work was obvious. But was he equal to it, nevertheless?

It is hard to say what he could or would have done. O'Neill's was a genius which functioned, as we have seen, in bitterness. Carlotta had removed the sources of friction which were shattering him as a man, if not as a writer. Only too promptly ill-health replaced the provocations of early hardship and ill-assorted marriage. He clung to his work in a convulsive effort to retain his dwindling powers.

His hands had always trembled. In moments of emotion they had shaken visibly. His mother's too, had done the same. At the conclusion of a week-long debauch, Agnes describes him as literally unable to lift a glass to his mouth. Indeed, the condition, which he attributed in some moods to past drinking, may have played its part in inducing him to give up liquor. Since then, it had grown gradually worse. Even in the first years of his new marriage, he had indulged himself in a special chair made to his design to aid his writing. Planned on the principle of a barber's chair, it had swinging shelves which brought books, paper and pencils, armrests, and so forth into easy reach. He had also decreased his handwriting to pinpoint size. The tiny letters were easier to form. But still the trembling increased.

Doctors prescribed a back brace which gave some relief. Temporary improvements in his physical condition helped also. But by 1943, when he was completing *A Moon for the Misbegotten*, there were actually times when he could not grasp a pencil.

He struggled grimly, desperate and terrified. He had made his writing into his whole life, and now . . . The doctors called his illness Parkinson's disease, incurable and progressive. He was only in the middle fifties, and his mind was perfectly sound. But the day was going to come when he could not write.

Carlotta wore out her eyes deciphering his wavering lines and typing him fair copies. This, however, could only put off the end. He tried dictating to her, but her presence was a distraction. It is often characteristic of writers who express themselves with difficulty that their work habits, as though to impose a pattern on their thoughts, are very rigid. O'Neill had to have his twelve pencils all sharpened and laid in a row. He had to have his paper just so, his other arrangements the same wherever he went. Besides, he was inarticulate. His voice had always been halting. He depended, no doubt, on a backward glance over what he had just written. At all events, the man who had given up his favorite vice, his friends, his family because they interfered with his writing, could not manage to use a dicta-phone, though future work depended on it. Even an electric typewriter was tried, unsuccessfully.

By the end of 1943, Carlotta was desperate. Servants had vanished into war work or the armed forces. The chauffeur in particular was indispensable. Eugene now trembled too much to drive, while she had never learned. A perfectionist, she could not let things go; and yet the cooking, the cleaning, the gardening were beyond her strength. They moved again, this time to an apartment in San Francisco. But there was one thing left which O'Neill still could do. His great concept was floundering, and it seemed probable it would never be finished now. But he had salvage left in the three plays he had written on episodes of his own past. These had possessed him at various times so strongly that he had put his main work aside in order to express his feelings. Notable among these was *The Iceman Cometh*, still unpublished.

In 1946, the war now over, civilian travel in privacy and comfort could be resumed. O'Neill's health at last permitted a move to New York. The Guild Theater was waiting eagerly to start rehearsals. It was a dozen years since their last new O'Neill.

He had turned his back long since on Greenwich Village, as he had on the docks and Jimmy-the-Priest's. Such places did not belong to his life with Carlotta. She ensconced him in a suite at the Barclay while she selected a penthouse. However, theatrical work not only raised his spirits but introduced him again to many people to whom he had been for years little more than a legend. Not all of these were connections of the theater. In particular, it brought him back into the lives of both his sons.

The tragedy of the new generation of the O'Neills, now to be played out, was a fitting conclusion to the gloom of *A Long Day's Journey*, and perhaps to the great cycle of plays which he never finished. With Oona her father had already quarreled. As a debutante in New York, Oona had attracted a blare of publicity precisely calculated to arouse her father's distaste. A visit to him in California, where she had gone to get into the movies, confirmed the impression. Oona at eighteen, unsure of herself but brash, had all the flippant defiance and smooth exterior of her kind. Carlotta put her down as calculating and hard, deliberately out to marry money. Within the year, her marriage to Charlie Chaplin burst into the papers with a sensationalism amounting to scandal. Charlie was now fifty-six, slightly older than her father, and at present in bad odor with the public. This was soon to be intensified by a scandalous paternity suit in which, it is fair to say, he was acquitted. It might well seem probable that the lowest mercenary motives had inspired Oona. This, however, proved not to be the case. Brought up without a father, Oona alone of the young O'Neills had found a substitute. Chaplin was personally a remarkable man with immense vitality. Their marriage was happy. But not even the arrival of grandchildren could soften O'Neill. He hardly mentioned Oona again, and few of his friends dared bring up her name in his presence. When he was near death, one of them brought him a letter from Oona. He put it aside, unread. It is difficult to resist the conclusion that it was not misjudgment of her nature which caused him to throw her off. It was the publicity he could not forgive. It vibrated on the nerves which had been tortured by the scandal of his own desertion of Agnes.

Be that as it may, he still maintained relations with his sons. Of Eugene Junior he had hitherto been proud. Indeed the young man appeared exactly the sort of son who would be congenial to him. He had done well at Yale, was now on the faculty, and had begun to make himself a reputation as a scholar. O'Neill had been happy to pay for his graduate studies and had respected abilities in a different line from his own. He had even enjoyed the young man's company. Young Eugene never inflicted this on him for too long and did not make emotional demands. Unhappily, however, it had begun to appear that the difficult temperament of the O'Neill's had descended to him after all. Two marriages had ended in divorce. Presently he quit Yale to free-lance on radio programs, moved to Greenwich Village, adopted a beard, bohemian ways, and left-wing opinions, was known to be drinking. His father's enthusiasm fell off somewhat, while Carlotta's declined notably. O'Neill saw less and less of his elder son.

O'Neill can hardly be blamed for this development. The young man was in his thirties. There was nothing significant his father could have done to help him as he started to go downhill. It is even impossible to tell whether a different childhood could have saved him. At least O'Neill had not been stingy in paying to cultivate the young man's talents. That these should be eventually extinguished by a suicide committed in a blur of alcohol and in the confusion of another love affair was a tragedy his father's intentions had not deserved. Yet, looking backward over the young man's life, it may be suspected that something more than temperament was at fault. Eugene Junior was set adrift before his birth, which his father heard about casually in a bar when the barman showed him the paper.

Young Shane O'Neill had never even offered promise. A problem in adolescence, a drifter since, he had recently married a girl hardly more practical than himself, with whom he was living in a walk-up, cold-water flat in slum conditions. The two were now summoned to dine in their father's luxurious suite at the Barclay.

Eugene had not much sympathy for Shane. He was Agnes's son, for one thing. Besides, Shane's helplessness in the face of life was a perpetual appeal to his father to take a hand. A succession of crises had resolved themselves by now into a succession of requests for loans. What Shane did with these, his father from experience could guess. He therefore denied them. But instead of pulling himself together, Shane sank lower.

This recent marriage seemed at least an encouraging sign. O'Neill was happy to be cordial. He and Carlotta pressed a bottle of good wine on the young pair. Later on, Carlotta made her way to the cold-water flat and presented a layette. These amenities did not seem much to the young couple, sensitive to the contrast between the two styles of living and hardly knowing at times where the next meal was coming from. But appeals for help only convinced O'Neill that the more he gave, the more would be demanded. Informed by young Mrs. O'Neill that Shane had been taken ill and that they were in desperate straits, he sent his lawyer and his doctor around to call. They arrived at an unfortunate moment. Shane had pulled himself together sufficiently to stagger off to a party in hopes of getting a decent meal. A friend, meanwhile, was sleeping off too many drinks on the vacated bed. The doctor and lawyer, neither of whom knew Shane by sight, fell on the wrong man with ludicrous results. O'Neill was furious, the incident adding to his dislike of getting involved.

The relationship limped along for a while. A third Eugene was born and bedded down in a bureau drawer. Here he managed to suffocate a few months later by sleeping on his face. It was an accident which might have happened in the most luxurious of cradles. The papers, however, found fresh sensation in the cold-water flat and the state of the baby. Its casual parents had not deliberately neglected it, but ignorance and helplessness and primitive conditions had left it with a bad case of diaper rash. When the grandson of a rich and famous man dies in such a condition, it is easy to imply he is at fault without suggesting precisely what he should have done. Agnes, interfering on behalf of the young parents, who were genuinely brokenhearted, appealed to O'Neill for funds to send them to the Bermuda house, which she still owned. They desperately needed time to get away and recover. It was O'Neill's chance to pay Agnes off. He put up the money and deducted every cent from the sum she lived on.

This ended relations with Shane. O'Neill seems to have felt, as he had done with Oona, that notoriety was the unforgivable sin. He was too old, too ill to cope with it. He needed his full strength for the daily battle his life had become. Perhaps he might have forgiven Shane for an accident which was no fault of his, had it not been for a further revelation some time later. The papers reported that Shane had been arrested for possession of drugs.

A drug-taker! Eugene had been through that once with his mother. He could not, would not face drugs over again. With a resolution only too characteristic, he put Shane out of his life. The death of young Eugene left him without children.

Even his relationship with Carlotta was sadly tainted by the gloom of his last years. He still loved her and, what was more, depended on her utterly. Yet as he sat help-lessly brooding in his house in Marblehead, the last of so many retreats, what was he to do? Could he sit forever watching the sea through his high-powered glasses? The policy of seeing none save by invitation, which he had carried on for so many years, left him lonely now. There was no variety of companionship to distract his mind. He found no outlet for his pent-up bitterness or for the drama which had always dominated his thinking. Carlotta, worn and nervous, racked with arthritis, was gallantly trying to smooth an existence which could not be smoothed any more. There was nothing left for him but to walk out, who knows in what rage or with what intentions? In such haste was he that he forgot his cane, without which he could barely walk a yard. On a bitter winter day he forgot his overshoes, his coat and hat. He took a few steps through eight inches of snow and stumbled, breaking his leg and fainting from the pain. He lay unconscious for perhaps an hour. Carlotta had been taking bromides to soothe nervous tension and had proved allergic to the drug. It had reduced her to a strange, confused state. She hardly knew what she was doing.

Soon he and Carlotta were in separate hospitals, both under treatment. It was Eugene's last dramatic scene, and he played it to the full. Friends were at his bedside, each receiving a differently colored account of his relation to Carlotta. Separation was talked of.

He went back to her in the end. Where else should he go? He was physically helpless, actually in debt. And he loved her. Carlotta was willing to nurse him with the old devotion. But the house in Marblehead was impractical now. They moved to a suite in a Boston hotel, where he hardly left his room, but spent his days staring at the river Charles, his last sight of water.

He was far beyond any work by now. He could not even tear up what still remained of his great unfinished cycle. Carlotta had to help his poor hands with the task. He had already in 1944 torn up the first four plays. The fifth, A Touch of the Poet, was also completed. He had preserved it, together with the sixth play, More Stately Mansions, five times as long as a regular play and still unpolished. Scenarios of five more existed also. These last he now destroyed, together with the current version of More Stately Mansions, though in this case he overlooked an earlier copy. This, with his notes on the cycle and "A Touch of the Poet," were all he left behind. A Touch of *the Poet* was performed after his death. It is an interesting, but not particularly successful play.

After this final destruction, he seemed to give up living. Soon a fever set in, but he had strength to raise himself and deliver a verdict on his life. "Born in a hotel room and—God damn it—died in a hotel room." It was true in more ways than one. He had never been at home in any place. Other people had all been transients to him. He died on November 27, 1953. He was sixty-five.

CRITICAL SUMMARY

THAT EUGENE O'NEILL was America's first great playwright none can deny. His achievement ranks with that of famous European dramatists. But what is his good work and what is his bad work seems less clear to many. Critics may be useful in pointing out values we have not seen for ourselves, but they have no right to destroy our powers of judgment. Since in O'Neill's case we cannot please everybody, there is no point in being timid about our own feelings. We can actually come to his plays with a fresh mind.

Diverse as the plays are, they group themselves into units which are roughly, though not entirely, chronological. Most controversial of these are what may be called the plays of the middle period, of which examples are *The Great God Brown, Lazarus Laughed, Strange Interlude.* Around these disputes swirl, and the verdict may tend to be a personal one. Either you like them or you do not. These three important plays and a number of others are what one may describe as ambitious plays. They are in the first place highly experimental. The use of masks in *Brown* and *Lazarus,* the enormous, almost pageant-like scale of the latter, the asides in *Strange Interlude,* its length—which imposes on us the effect of an entire novel at one sitting—all these are new techniques, if not invented, at least developed by O'Neill. But interesting though these experiments are, they merely represent symbols of an urge to pierce through the form of our lives as well as of the drama. What they are saying is what all three plays are saying: "What is life about?"

Most people will agree that O'Neill found no ultimate answer which satisfied him for long or will satisfy us. But he said himself at one time that he hoped to be a failure because a man should not be content with what was in his reach. Measured by this remark, his most ambitious plays may well be his greatest because they express the boldness of his spirit in many different ways. To those who admire this group, *Mourning Becomes Electra* is the greatest of O'Neill's plays and one of the very great plays of all time. It may not appear to belong with these others, but it does so because of the effort with which O'Neill lifts the Mannon tragedy onto the level of a great story of the ages. Its scale, too, gives it an aspiring, epic quality. Though not quite in the same sense a play with a message, it digs deep into human nature, even into human history, reaching inward where *Lazarus* and *Brown* reach outward.

Other people, unimpressed, maintain that *Brown* and *Lazarus* are less lofty than pretentious. They often attempt to convince by mere repetition. O'Neill is not a thinker and has nothing new to say on a philosophical subject. The plot of *Strange Interlude* would look naïve in a novel. Its asides are nearly all dull; one or two of its scenes fall almost comically flat; and some of its psychology is more like a handbook than anything deeply felt. In any case, O'Neill does not understand the middle classes. He is not sensitive to their complex motives. He has no ear for their language and no natural eloquence of his own. *Mourning Becomes Electra,* however impressive, depends for effect on Greek drama and for profundity on Freud. In other words, O'Neill is sharing in works for which he cannot claim credit. He tortures his plot to make it fit the original more or less, and his clumsiness of expression is a strange contrast to the deathless poetry of which he seeks to remind us. In fact, to critics of this kind, the most readable plays of the middle period are the two introductory ones, *The Emperor Jones* and *The Hairy Ape.* Shorter and less ambitious than the rest, they succeed through their very limitations.

Dismissing, then, the ambitious plays, this group of critics goes back to the realism which originally impressed the Provincetown Players. Here, they say, is the true talent of O'Neill. They admit his temptation to sentimentality in the *S.S. Glencairn* dramas. Nevertheless, these are vivid representations, as are *Diff'rent, Beyond the Horizon,* and others. All are shorter, less repetitious, not overcharged with second-hand ideas. At his best, O'Neill is a writer whose tremendous emotions and melodramatic sense have extraordinary power. *Desire Under the Elms* is for such critics the greatest drama that O'Neill ever wrote.

So far, so good; but there is a third controversy about the value of the last plays, mainly *The Iceman Cometh* and *Long Day's Journey Into Night.* It is obvious that these are a retreat from experimentation and a looking backward into O'Neill's personal past. Bleakly pessimistic, they not merely abandon the quest for eternal values but insist that there are none. For this reason, those who admire the aspiring O'Neill will find in these a terrible falling away. They are plays of illness and old age, even though both were finished before the worst years had come upon him.

The last plays, then, do not find favor with the supporters of *Electra.* But the school of *Desire Under the Elms* is not unanimously approving either. To admirers of the brilliant construction of that stark tragedy, *The Iceman* is dreadfully verbose. In rehearsal, it was pointed out to O'Neill, who always hated criticism, that he had made the same point eighteen times. "I *meant* it to be repeated eighteen times!" was his savage self-defense. This is no excuse, even if true. Besides, the episodes of the minor characters are mere illustrations of the theme, not parts of the action. Transpose the dialogue in blocks, and the play will run along equally well. Finally, the monologue of Hickey at the end is out of all reasonable proportion and almost unplayable because of its length. Less verbose, *Long Day's Journey* is simply pointless. One starts and ends nowhere. A piece of biography, it hardly forms a unit.

In spite of these faults, and they are very grave ones, the defenders of the last two plays also have sound reasons. They base their argument on O'Neill's ability to portray and rouse emotion. This none deny; and looked at from this angle, it is possible to judge these plays as great without bothering to defend them in detail. Free from the sickening sentiment of *A Moon for the Misbegotten*, they have their message for the human heart. And in the character of Larry, who was old Terry Carlin, O'Neill permits himself a compassion which is rare.

Larry hints at another side of O'Neill which he shows us seldom. What about *Ah, Wilderness!?* Can O'Neill, then, do nothing but portray the tragic emotions? *Ah, Wilderness!* is an amusing and tender comedy. Sentimental it may be, but delightfully so. The play is more than a reflection of the sentiment of *In the Zone* or *A Moon for the Misbegotten*. It is actually evidence that O'Neill possessed some sense of humor. One can see other signs of this in minor episodes and bits of dialogue in various plays, but humor never dominates the stage, except in this one case. The fact is, despite O'Neill's inner gloom, he had a sense of enjoyment and fun. Though never naturally high-spirited, he did not strike his friends as a humorless person. It was merely that his humor was quiet and limited in scope. It did not dominate his nature. In *Ah, Wilderness!*

he permits himself a smile over the follies of an adolescence which he well remembers. To enjoy it without bitterness, he sets it against the background of a typical anxious mother, well-meaning father, lordly, careless elder brother. *Ah, Wilderness!* was written at great speed. If it had not been so, O'Neill's mood might have broken. Although genuinely part of himself, it is hardly a characteristic play.

It is easy to point out great faults in O'Neill's writings, yet despite them he dominated his generation. He may have deserved to because of his merits, which were also great. As it happened, however, he was one of those fortunate writers who are truly concerned with the problems of their age. One may compare him in this respect with Edna St. Vincent Millay. Her talent no one questions. Her interest in many things vital to her times was deep. She was never able, for instance, to shut out World War II, as did O'Neill. Yet the publication of Eliot's *The Waste Land* made Miss Millay suddenly and disastrously old-fashioned. No such situation overtook O'Neill. He seemed to embody in his unhappy youth and childhood the distinctive tendencies of our century—loss of faith, rootlessness, general, almost aimless rebellion. Deliberately reducing himself to the level of those who had lost ambition and hope, he yet survived to tell the tale. Obsessed by a need for self-expression, he was dominated by it no less completely than his characters are by hate, greed, passion, love, or fear. His work made him; and to it he sacrificed his life, his friends, his love, his very vices. In fact, he poured everything into his writing with lopsided passion. This is, as he truly understood, typical of people who have lost the familiar guidelines of religion, convention, and traditional culture. His heroes meet their fate unaided by such things. Lavinia Mannon shuts herself up to face her family ghosts alone.

For such a character as O'Neill, success was vital. His was not a genius which would flower unseen. Too many destructive forces in him were ready to take revenge for disappointment. Besides, his tastes and his nature were dramatic. He must be better or worse than other people. The Provincetown Players gave him years of encouragement which he might otherwise not have received. Without them, it is hard to tell whether he would have continued to struggle or sunk back into the depths. In any case, it is clear he would not have developed so rapidly and surely without a stage, an acting company, and an appreciative audience. For O'Neill learned his theatrical skill in the theater, more completely than any other dramatist but Shakespeare. Brought up in a family where details of acting or management were commonplace subjects, he had the good fortune to mature in an experimental age. It was not merely the nature of drama that was in question, but all the techniques of production as well. Changes in stage design, in the plastic arts, in music were affecting the whole concept of dramatic art. Imagination was as busy with stage effects as with playwriting.

For those who would make new dramatic rules, experience is essential. Ideas must pass the test of production. They must seem valuable to the cast, which learns to know them well, and to the audience, which presumably is a fresh one every night. They must prove practicable within the limitations of the theater. They must, besides, fall into true proportion, forwarding the action and never obscuring what the playwright wishes to say. It was experience which the Provincetown gave to O'Neill. Without the little theatre, it is hard to see how he could have learned his craft as well.

It is easy, as we have already seen, to pick holes in O'Neill's plays. He was guilty of shallow melodrama, garrulousness, inordinate length, and half a dozen other failings, any one of which would have ruined a lesser man. Yet in production and on the stage the world accepted him on his own terms. It still accepts him.

Two things, then, the Provincetown Playhouse contributed to the making of the first great American dramatist. It gave him an atmosphere in which he could work, saving him from the abyss which waited for him. It polished a superb technical mastery and developed his willingness to experiment with new effects. *The Emperor Jones,* high point of the Provincetown's existence, is at the same time a crown of its endeavors. With these things in mind, it is fair to say Cook and the Provincetown Players made O'Neill.

They made him and did not make him. They had nothing to do with his genius or his tortured experience. *Bound East for Cardiff,* written before they discovered him, is as typical of his work as *Emperor Jones.* Indeed, it would be impossible to imagine Eugene O'Neill as being as plastic in the hands of Jig as, for instance, Susan Glaspell.

It would be far more true to say that O'Neill seized on the Players to further his own ends; and that when they had done so, he cast them off forever. A man with a great passion, he was not bound by tradition or shaped by Cook's ideals. He was in all experiences Eugene O'Neill.

LIST OF MAJOR PLAYS

PLAYS OF REALISM

S.S.Glencairn Plays	1916–18
Beyond the Horizon	1920
Anna Christie	1921
Desire Under the Elms	1924

PLAYS OF EXPERIMENT

The Emperor Jones	1920
The Hairy Ape	1922
The Great God Brown	1926
Strange Interlude	1928
Mourning Becomes Electra	1931

COMEDY

Ah, Wilderness!	1933

LAST PLAYS

The Iceman Cometh	1946
Long Day's Journey Into Night	1955

Dates are date of first performance, which generally follows not too long after completion, except for "The Iceman Cometh," written in 1939, and "Long Day's Journey Into Night," written in 1939–1941.

INDEX